THE TRICK

THE TRICK

Why Some People Can Make Money
and Other People Can't

WILLIAM LEITH

BLOOMSBURY PUBLISHING

LONDON · OXFORD · NEW YORK · NEW DELHI · SYDNEY

BLOOMSBURY PUBLISHING
Bloomsbury Publishing Plc
50 Bedford Square, London, WC1B 3DP, UK

BLOOMSBURY, BLOOMSBURY PUBLISHING and the Diana logo are trademarks
of Bloomsbury Publishing Plc

First published in Great Britain 2020

A catalogue record for this book is available from the British Library

ISBN: HB: 978-0-7475-9940-1; TPB: 978-1-5266-1987-7; EBOOK: 978-1-4088-3418-3

2 4 6 8 10 9 7 5 3 1

Typeset by Newgen KnowledgeWorks Pvt., Ltd, Chennai, India
Printed and bound in Great Britain by CPI Group (UK) Ltd, Croydon CR0 4YY

To find out more about our authors and books visit www.bloomsbury.com
and sign up for our newsletters

To my parents

I

It's like I actively want to be poor.

Like I'd *rather* be poor.

Like everything I do, consciously or unconsciously, is to say: hey, poverty, come over here, I love you.

These are my waking thoughts on the day I discover the secret of making millions.

Fifty miles away, in Chelsea Harbour, Jordan Belfort is waiting for me in a hotel I have never seen, but which I imagine as white, with big glass panels.

Yes, that's right – Jordan Belfort. The man who calls himself, or at least his book about himself, *The Wolf of Wall Street*.

I'm not sure about that title.

If I were him, and if I wrote a book about how I made millions, and then realised that having millions makes you feel poor, if I wrote a book like that, about feeling poor and devising a fraud and getting caught and going to jail, I can't see myself calling it *The Wolf of Wall Street*.

I'd call it something else. I don't know what, exactly.

But the point is, the book is about how some people can make money and some people can't, a subject that fascinates me, and injects pure cold anxiety directly into my stomach.

I've never told anyone this, but I have a mental disorder in the area of finance. I am driven by a mechanism designed to prevent me from being rich; worse, it masquerades as a mechanism designed to do exactly the opposite.

It is an enemy agent, it lies deep in the wiring of my brain, and I don't know how it works.

I know I need to dismantle this mechanism and replace it with a new one, before I die a pauper's death. But I'm terrified of doing this, because I suspect that the mechanism is, actually, me.

Money is weird, anyway. We're supposed to instinctively understand it. But we really don't. For instance, most people think it's real. It's not. But because we *think* it's real, it's real. It somehow emerged from the early murk of human interaction. It trumps God, because you can't make God exist just by thinking he exists. He either exists or he doesn't. But money is different.

It is *us*. It's our masterpiece. It's killing us.

So anyway, how can a guy whose relationship with money is, basically, that it destroys him, it's even on the cover of his book, 'how money destroyed a Wall Street superstar' – how can a guy like that call himself the Wolf of anything?

Particularly Wall Street, the Hub of Money.

Because he wasn't the Wolf of the Hub of Money, was he? If you went in the ring with Mike Tyson, and Tyson destroyed you, would you then call yourself the Wolf of Mike Tyson?

These are my second, third and fourth thoughts on the day I find the secret of how to make millions. As you can see, they are not, so far, positive thoughts.

I'm thinking that maybe the Wolf is not Jordan Belfort. Maybe it's not a person at all. Maybe the Wolf is *money itself*.

I should ask him. Or I should ask Martin Scorsese. I know that Scorsese is making a film about Belfort, and I know he's calling it *The Wolf of Wall Street*, and I can see it, can see what he'll do with the story, can see the arc of aspiration, the nervous and vicious laughter, the bad words, the dirty words, the fast talk, the money talk. Leonardo diCaprio, with the charisma of a fallen angel, will play Belfort.

As these sparks rise and fall through the dark sky of my half-alert mind I'm stretching my arm out and batting my fingers around, trying to locate my alarm clock, which is bleeping. Being late today would be ruinous.

There are two things I must remember this morning, because I wrote them down on a piece of paper, and put it on my bedside table.

I'm interviewing Belfort for a magazine. That's how I make money. I interview people – almost exclusively the rich and the super-rich. (Mostly men, by the way, for about a million reasons.) I persuade these people to talk about themselves – not as easy as it sounds. My mission is always to extract their secrets, to reveal their modus operandi, to travel upstream into the darkness of their hearts, and then to assassinate them – not quite with extreme prejudice, but in a nuanced sort of way. To reveal their inner pain. Tears are my pot of gold.

Anyway, before I meet the people I interview, I try to understand what motivates them. I think about what it's like to *be* them. I take notes. I edit the notes. I boil everything down to the basics.

Hence the piece of paper. I peer at it in the half-light of my room. It says:

1 How he made the money
2 Why he turned to crime

Rolling the paper into a ball, and aiming it at the far wall of my bedroom, I slump back down on my pillow. The ball falls short. My other hand finds the clock.

The bleeping stops.

I *must* dismantle the mechanism before it's too late. But I think the mechanism might be me.

What if it's me?

***

In the silence, I consider my own financial situation. Just thinking about it, I am sick with dread, icy dread spreading up from my stomach into my chest and neck, and now I can't stop thinking about it, the bad thoughts and feelings are seeping out and getting everywhere, it's like a crime scene I must clean up before I can even begin to get away, and the more I try to clean it, the dirtier it gets.

But I must *not* think like this!

OK. My financial situation. Like most nation states, I'm currently running a deficit – in other words, my life is costing me more money than I make. A deficit – it's not the same as a debt. A deficit is from the spending you're doing now, and will be punished for in the future. A debt is from the spending you did in the past. It's the punishment you're already taking.

I'm aware that I've asked for this punishment – this *abuse*. It is happening to me because, on one level, I must want the abuse to happen to me.

I hate it. I can't even think about it. But I *have to*. But I *can't*.

But I *must*.

I am being abused by secured and unsecured loans, unpaid bills and taxes, fines, penalty fees, pending court cases, and cases I have already lost, or not contested, or forgotten about. The cases come back as different types of letters, with this or that tone, and then as actual people, again mostly men, not well dressed, they particularly have no idea about shoes. When they come, these men (and occasionally women), I am very polite indeed. I serve tea and offer food. I think it makes a difference.

I am driven by a desire to spend more money than I have, so I borrow money, from banks and corporations and individuals, and I don't pay it back promptly, because in truth I never had a strong desire to pay it back, I just wanted the money. The money actually makes me feel younger and healthier. It buys me time. Do you think I want to pay it back?

I know I have an obligation to pay it back. I should pay it back. But I'm not sure I *must* pay it back. Why must I pay it back?

To be clear: I *intend* to, but I don't *want* to. And so people come to my house. We talk, and all is quiet for a while.

Give me time, I tell them.

***

Look, I'm not a money kind of person. Growing up, I was too privileged to think very much about money. Now things have changed – now the tide has gone out – I'm not privileged enough not to.

I have fallen through the cracks. It's nobody's fault. Yes it is. It's mine.

It's my fault.

***

My work. I sell stories to magazines. But, when I do this, I'm not exactly selling the story to the readers. I'm actually selling the readers to advertisers – a dirty trick. A further abuse. What I'm selling, to be exact, is the attention of my readers. That precious thing. When I tell a story, I'm actually priming my readers for the main event – getting them ready for the moment they cast eyes on the beautiful, shiny ads.

I'm saying, I know you'll be interested in this person I've talked to. But also: why not check this out, over here! Look at these amazing cars. The chrome and steel. The fat tyres. Look at these watches. Look at this white sand beach, this crystal sea.

And look at the pictures of women. Sifted and selected by money's cruel artistry.

The point of view is not male or female, not his or hers. It's money's.

Just for a moment, let these images penetrate your field of vision. These women, they have this perfect flesh! It's so smooth and firm! And the angles of nose, cheek, pelvis and thigh, these acute angles, mathematically speaking, will beguile you. Gaze at these very specific human faces and bodies; doing this for just a second will set in motion a chain reaction of hormones in your brain and body, whether your gaze is male or female.

Take them in, these images. You will experience a suite of emotions: yearning, envy, pique, spite, rage, self-doubt, shame, nostalgia, ambition. Tiny taps will turn on inside you, will seep and squirt, will marginally alter the composition of your blood.

Sometimes I am well paid. But well paid is not the same as rich. It's not even base camp.

I don't *only* interview rich people. If I made a pie-chart of how I spend my time, there'd be one slice to represent interviewing rich people. There'd be a slice for sitting in cafes. There'd be a slice for walking around with no specific destination in mind.

The rest, the Pac-Man-shaped lion's share of the chart, is a blur. I sit around, or lie around, often in or on my bed, and read books. I develop obsessions – like how apes turned into people. Everyone knows they did that. But *how*, exactly, did they do that?

And how did they build my world – the modern world? Which, of course, like every other world, will collapse, and turn to ruins, and become the ancient world.

Like everybody else in history, we see ourselves as modern. But we're not. We're ancient.

I could have been a philosopher.

Oh please. Not this again.

Anyway, I learned to speed-read twenty-odd years ago; now I get through a book a day, and often more.

I'm looking for something, and I can't stop looking, but I never find what I'm looking for.

Meanwhile my deficit grows. And my debts. My punishment. Which I don't want to think about.

Because it makes me feel sick.

My punishment – I keep it at the edge of my consciousness. But it's always there.

It waits. It creeps up.

It's a strange noise in an empty house. It's a face at the window on a dark night.

***

My phone is buzzing. Did I fall asleep? I must not be late today – must not! I move up onto my elbows. I need to act, and fast.

OK.

How he made the money.

Why he turned to crime.

This, the crime, troubles me. As far as I can see, Jordan Belfort made tens of millions of dollars. Which made him feel he *did not have enough money.* It made him feel poor. So he devised a fraud, a crime, which seemed like the perfect crime, but wasn't, because he got caught and went to jail.

So if he had an enormous amount of money, and it still wasn't enough, there must have been a moment of slippage, a moment when his mind went wrong, and I'm sure that this phenomenon, this psychological black ice, was caused by the money.

Money is *not simple.* It's both real and not real. The moment you have it, you can't see it, because it's in you, it's part of you.

It is magic. It is witchcraft. It can be in two places at once.

I think I know where it started, by the way. It started at the exact moment, around two million years ago, when an ape looked at a forest fire and had a new type of thought.

The ape sees the fire. The right side of his brain processes the information.

Fire.

And then …

And then, for the first time in the history of the world, the left side of the ape's brain, the aspirational left side, takes the information, grasps it, and does something new with it.

Why not poke a stick into the fire? Then, surely, you can make more fire.

You can get *something for nothing.*

That can't be true! But it must be true! It's …

***

My phone is buzzing again. It's set to buzz every two minutes. On the third round of buzzing, my second backup alarm, my Chelsea clock, will start to bleep. I really should have an Arsenal clock, because Arsenal is my team, but for some reason I've got a Chelsea clock – Chelsea, owned by a Russian billionaire, rather than Arsenal, owned by a slightly poorer Russian billionaire. Russians – caged for so long, they are better predators than the rest of us. They are hungrier. They have sharper teeth.

Anyway, in the old days, you hoped that money might help your team to win. Now, you hope winning will help your team to make money. Money used to be a facilitator for the game. Now it *is* the game. Marx said that. Obviously not about football. But he saw it coming.

Next: coffee? If there's time. But I don't even have time to finish my train of thought about apes, let alone boil a kettle, let it stand a while, like thirty seconds, while I'm arranging the ground beans, the cafetiere, the spoonful of honey.

I only ever have two types of time: far, far too much time for my own good, and then almost no time at all – relentlessly needing to shave seconds off every personal action.

I should set up a time exchange, buying time from the poor, who are often time-rich, and then selling it to the rich, who are usually time-poor, because having money eats up time like nothing else, it really does. Time exchange – a brilliant idea, with global implications, perhaps. The dumbest idea in the world, perhaps.

Which is it? I genuinely can't tell.

Almost fully awake now, running my fingers upwards through my hair. Hard objects are on, and in, the bed – books. Damaged with love like old teddy bears. *How to Get Rich* by Felix Dennis. *Touching the Void* by Joe Simpson. Men who climbed and fell.

Also Nassim Taleb, Patrick Veitch, Richard Wrangham, Aaron Brown, Matt Ridley.

My imaginary colleagues.

I swing my legs out, make contact with something – a water bottle. Feet on the wet carpet. Not unpleasant.

More thoughts: why am I not on a tropical island, in a luxury cabin, or lounging on a terrace with my feet in a plunge pool, reading a bestseller? Or, for that matter, *writing* a bestseller. Why not *writing* a bestseller?

A familiar thought. I edit it.

Beep-beep. The Chelsea clock.

***

And I'm up. Four minutes in the shower. I need a new bathroom. I hate the one I've got. I want, I need, I *want*, the spoiled brat in me *wants* a new bathroom, I want the newness and shine, the shine of the tiles, the shine of the glass, the panels of glass, that's what I want, but what does *I want* get? I want gets a smacked bottom.

Or does it?

I'm pretty sure that in the future, a rich person's alarm clock won't shock them into wakefulness, but set in motion a silent machine designed to convey them along a production line, as they sleep, moving them towards a siphon for the bladder, a gentle but comprehensive enema, a soaping, rinsing and drying process, plus a robot to arrange clothes, deodorant, hair products and so on, everything in exactly the right order, a just-in-time machine, designed to perfection, so the first thing you'll be aware of, the thing that actually wakes you up, will be the smell of frying bacon, or toast; you'll open your eyes to find yourself already at the breakfast table. I'd like to be the person who patents *that* invention.

My mind is clearing. I am currently sober. I have not been sleeping well.

Back to the bedroom. The bed a smashed nest, the floor a rink of glossy magazines. I stand, dripping, looking for a clean towel. I have all these semi-clean towels. I know one or two of them have, in the recent past, been wet, on the floor, absorbing stuff from the floor, for *days*, particles from my shoes, spores or whatever, and if I had more time I could try to work out which towels are the dirty towels and which the clean, but I don't have time, so I must take a risk, I must gamble, and the problem with this is that I don't like to think of myself as a gambler – which might, actually, be the main reason I don't have millions.

The towels. Five or six of them. Still dripping, I look at them, and for a moment I'm lost, have no idea what to do, am completely, utterly frozen.

That's when I hear the knock on the door.

It's a guy.

He's shouting.

'Taxi!'

***

At the station, I pay with my card. A bead of liquid is running down the edge of my eye socket. The guy behind the glass says something, he's mumbling. There's a slight tightening in the chest as I imagine the intimate data on my card being relayed down the wires, and, for the briefest instant, I can't help cursing the fact that I don't have several top-notch cards, that I don't have a roll of banknotes in my pocket, that I don't own my house outright, that I hate my bathroom, that I can't afford, say, the best dental treatment money can buy.

I travel second class, and this must have some psychological significance, the fact that there are two classes, and my assumption, from the start, is that I will travel in the poorer of these two classes. Asking for the poorer seats is my default setting.

Not that I mind the actual *seats*. It's not the *seats*.

I can feel the people behind me, shuffling and breathing, their patience filed down to the minimum, self-loathing bubbling away, fists balling, teeth grinding, you're never far from a rupture of the social fabric. Which reminds me of a female passenger who got off the train two stops down the line, and jumped over the wall at the edge of the platform, beyond which was a wood. Had she disappeared into the wood? No. She came back with two large rocks, and threw the rocks, one at a time, at the windows of the train. The windows buckled and crazed, but did not break. People flinched. I flinched. Each time she threw a rock, the woman let out a tennis-player's howl. In tennis, people call it grunting. But it's more like howling. The woman went over the wall again and came back with another rock. She threw the rock at the train. Again, the window buckled and crazed, but did not break.

My card, I'm thinking.

Why do I flirt with poverty? I don't know, but I must know, deep down, must have the knowledge, but I don't want to let it into the conscious part of my brain, so I recycle the thought, a familiar track; why do I flirt with poverty, why do I sidle up to it, say sweet and dirty things to it, why do I invite it into my house, my life? I don't know, but I must know, but I don't want to think about it, but I *do*, I *do* want to think about it, just not now, not now.

Turns out I've missed the train that would have made for the ideal, unhurried journey. But I can still, just about, make my appointment.

The guy is handling my card, manhandling it, feeding it into a machine, feeding me, my details, into a machine, so the machine can see into the murk of my financial soul – the volatile comings and goings, the sudden cascades of pluses and minuses, the windfalls, the impulse buys – the machine knows about the time last week when I just couldn't wait for the bus a moment longer, I'd had it, and my arm went up, and I was swept away, from the people and the dirt, the dirt, the people, the taxi feeling like an airlift, a mountain rescue, the subsequent half-hour journey costing me a poor person's weekly budget.

The machine *knows*.

The machine is not stupid, it is smart, it is a psychiatrist, a mathematician, an observer and collator of tiny details. It *knows*. It knows me better than I know myself.

It knows about the anxiety, the neurosis, the days spent in bed. It knows about the war on alcohol – the truces and ceasefires, the skirmishes and massacres. And it knows about the secret desires, too – knows that I want to get away from the dirt and the people, that I want to live in the good part of town, protected by some kind of electrified fence, possibly even guards, but no, because guards turn on you, so just locks, please, and a lovely view, a perfect bathroom, shiny.

The despicable desires.

I'm watching the machine as it sucks and licks my card, one of its billion little tongues darting through the ether, the tip of the cyber tongue touching my card, telling the monstrous cyber brain what my card tastes like. I'm grinding the rim of one of my molars into the tooth below.

I look at the guy. The guy looks at me. He gives me a look.

The machine says yes. My card tastes good.

Yes!

Some good news. My card is sweet. Some bad news: I'm inching closer to the time when it will turn rotten. As I slide it into my wallet,

as I push it into the leather slit, the card feels light, insubstantial.
I see that the signature, the mark of my professional hand, has been
almost completely worn away.

But I'm expecting some money! Money is coming towards me!
Someone will touch a key, and the money will move towards me
at close to the speed of light, and hundreds of people will try
to slow it down as it moves, to touch it or hold it for a while,
because if you can touch or hold it for even a moment, a tiny
bit will stick to you, a few microscopic flakes, and if you spend
your whole life trying to touch money as it comes past, you will
collect a lot of flakes.

It will come! One day, I will be inundated. That's what I tell
myself. At this middle stage in my life, I still feel as if there is
money close by, possibly even inside me, locked away somewhere,
deep inside my brain.

The mechanism!

If I wanted to, I could dismantle the mechanism. If I *wanted*
to. Anybody can be rich if they want to. That's what Felix Dennis
says. But you have to understand what he means by *wanting to*. He
means being *obsessed*. By a desire that is almost sociopathic. You
must be beyond ruthless. Your first victim will be yourself. You will
reach inside your own head and hold the mechanism in your hands
and take it apart, unravelling the wires one by one like a bomb
disposal expert.

Not happy thoughts, as I walk down the dirty station stairs on
this particular day, the day I will be exposed to the secret of how
people make millions.

***

Belfort. I have to get him clear in my head. I need to make
him mine.

My God – what if I don't?

But I will, I will.

I will look back and say: today was the turning point. The day
I picked myself up. Like in the Bible: 'Take up thy bed and walk.'
Well, I will *run*. Take up thy bed and *run*.

There's the other possibility, of course. I've seen it so many times. I will become one of those shuffling people, red-faced, appalling, the life and soul of some smelly old bar.

I know, I know, my mind is drifting, escaping its task, my eyes now scanning the platform, the men with jackets and ties, holding raincoats. Above it's grey and black with bolts of white light.

So. Belfort. Grew up in an apartment in Bayside, Queens. His father an accountant, a formal dresser, a smoker. His mother strict, a checker of homework. One brother, no sister. They were not poor. But being not poor demanded struggle, hard work, keeping one's nose clean, allowing the world to process you, the respectable world, it's all about being obedient, you do what you're told, you climb the ladder. But Belfort is clever, he's bolshie, he wants more than this. He doesn't just want to climb the ladder. He wants to climb a mountain. A mountain of money. He wants the mansion and the lawn, the bathroom and the view, the cars and the boats, the private flights, the perfect women, the chunky watches you see in the pages of the glossy magazines.

His dad – yes, that's right, his dad was grumpy, I guess didn't enjoy life much, a man of routines, put his jacket and shoes on in the mornings and walked around in boxer shorts, fully dressed except for the trousers, then put the trousers on at the last moment, his one eccentricity, sounds like a cry for help.

The young Belfort wanted to walk around in boxer shorts all the time, not just for a pathetic few minutes in the morning. That's not quite true. But hold the thought. That guy, American Apparel, what's his name, Dov – yes, Dov Charney. He actually did that, became the multi-millionaire boss and wandered around the workplace in his underwear.

But Belfort – yes, *sort* of like that; he wanted control, wanted to make his own rules. Handsome but short. Pretty face. Blue eyes. Highly intelligent. Girls liked him. He's one of those guys, I know the type exactly, who always needs to have a pretty girl. As he gets more successful the girl has to be beautiful – must be a knockout. Married early, to a pretty girl, then dumped her for a beautiful girl, a model, Nadine Caridi, actually a top model, the Miller Lite girl on the TV ad.

And when he had money he had sex with lots of prostitutes – dozens, maybe hundreds. Ask him about that. He *understands* prostitutes. I should call them sex workers. Or sex brokers. Sex professionals. He called them hookers. What they do is: they turn tricks. The trick is to exploit a market that others do not acknowledge. They see a need that others do not want to see. They understand hidden needs because they have hidden needs themselves. They are dowsers of unseen supply and demand.

Belfort admitted to being unfaithful to his wife, but only with professionals. Only for money.

He's mercenary, he's the money personality, sees everything in terms of quantified transactions. Thinks he can buy anything.

Maybe that's not quite right.

He knows exactly what he can and can't buy.

That's not right either.

He *thought* he knew what he could and could not buy, and, as he got richer, the distinction became more elusive; in the end he couldn't see it.

That's right.

***

My train comes clunking in. I'm at the door, holding my man-bag. The hiss of the door. Inside, the poorer seats. Sun in my eye. People fussing over jackets, magazines. Glossy pages catching light like mirrors. Devices purring and beeping. Instructions from an alien intelligence.

My stomach feels cold. The train looks like it's moving, but it's an optical illusion, and then it starts actually to move, and when I'm sure beyond all doubt it's really moving I look around and feel myself start to relax, a moment of nirvana, everything will be good, my mind's eye filled with images of planes, cars, watches, shoes, perfect faces and bodies, fat tyres, palm trees, beaches, clear blue island sea.

OK then. Belfort started his own stockbroking firm, Stratton Securities, great name, and he moved to Lake Success, even better name, and he hired brokers, first a few, and then tens, and then hundreds, and they became a gang, a cult, a merry band, and they were heavy consumers of the services of sex workers, and they divided the sex workers into three categories.

The best they called blue chip, like the most expensive stocks. The next rung down was Nasdaqs, like the up-and-coming tech stocks. The lowest category was pink sheets, like the stocks not listed on the exchange, but printed on pink paper – the cheap stocks.

You could say Belfort had sex with blue-chip hookers, paid for by selling pink-sheet stocks. Sort of gross. I could say that. But no, probably not.

And he liked his brokers to splurge all their money, to get a taste for the cars and the watches and the women, he liked them to spend because spending made them need more money, which made them keener salesmen.

***

Rolling through villages now. Fields, cows, a barn: farming. A racecourse: gambling.

Now, let's see, I have a handy formula, filed away somewhere, where is it? Ah, OK. Money, the bedrock of our society, is debt, because it arrives in the economy in the form of loans.

And loans are based on interest, on *interest rates*.

And interest rates are based on the understanding of *risk*, the probability that something will happen, in this case how likely the borrower is to default on the loan.

And the concept of probability is often expressed in the form of *odds*.

So money, the thing that underpins our whole society, is a concept based on odds, and therefore gambling.

So gambling is the bedrock of society.

And what Aaron Brown says, he's like the high priest of risk analysis, he's a friend of Nassim Taleb, the guy who wrote *The Black Swan*; what Brown says is this. *Of course* our whole society is based on gambling. This is something all rich people know, they're all essentially gamblers, and lots of poor people are gamblers too, rich people often being good gamblers, and poor people mostly bad gamblers.

It's all gambling.

But the middle classes – the clean people – don't see this, or don't want to see it, or don't see it until it's too late, and I wish I wasn't one of them, one of the clean people, but deep down I think I am.

***

The tea trolley. The tea-trolley girl. Tall. Ukrainian? Polish? Her grandmother slept with Nazis – I bet. Someone from the night shift is drooling on her pillow right now. I'm trying to tune in the younger Belfort. The snap judgements. The acid tongue. He always had names for things, and those names were not kind. 'The Witch', 'The Devil', 'Pond Scum', 'Stinkoslovakia'. Not kind, but kind of on the money.

I ask for coffee. I think about chocolate. I should have a sandwich, but no, actually, because if you look at the ingredients I'm guessing it's as bad as chocolate anyway, sugar and starch and unholy fat, plus some crushed-up bits of egg from maybe Thailand or Korea, who knows, one bite and you start thinking about epidemics, bird flu, vast stinking warehouses full of them, the diseased beaks and tiny skulls, eyes like bits of grit, herky-jerky, cages rattling like a nightmare. When I was a reporter I wrote a story about a Korean revenge killer who worked in a chicken factory; he killed rival chick sexers. I met their families, and – I guess because they asked me to, or maybe expected me to – I knelt down and prayed with them, they were Christians, and afterwards I felt like I'd exploited them, and I'm still not sure if I did, but I *felt* like I did. This was the second time I'd written about murder, and the last. I really thought I'd write more about murder. I mean, *murder*. But there it is.

We are *rattling* along. With luck, I can still be on time. Or that other thing, which is to be not quite *bang* on time, but very close, so that your minor tardiness is soon forgotten, or perhaps even appreciated – that three- or four-minute lag that speaks of coolness, almost as if you're giving the other person a gift, the gift of your very slight lateness. *I'm not impeccable*, you're saying. I won't judge you if you don't judge me. I'm not that drill instructor type of person, you're saying. Not a martinet of punctuality. And think what punctuality actually means – it means a punch, from the Latin *punctum*. Boosh! A fist! In your *face*.

We slow down. We stop. The platform where they arrested the woman. The wall she climbed over. The woods beyond, where she found the rocks. We move off. We pick up speed. Past hedgerows. Past more trees.

Trees.

Holding the thought of the Korean revenge killer, I try to imagine what it would be *like* to be a prehistoric ape. You'd be in the trees. You *need* to live in the trees, in order to escape from the predators that live lower down – the lions, the tigers, with their sabre teeth. And then you learn to control fire, which means you don't need to live in the trees any more; now you can live on the ground, protected by the fire.

Now you don't need fur.

You learn to cook. Centuries pass. You learn to farm. You learn to farm intensively. Somebody, some chicken farmer in Taiwan or Korea, discovers that, if you separate the male chicks from the female chicks the moment they hatch, you can save money. A new profession is born: chick-sexing.

There's a college in Seoul where you can do a degree in chick-sexing. You spend three years learning how to tell a male chick from a female chick – in, like, a fraction of a second. They're on a conveyor belt, coming towards you. Thousands of them. Your hand–eye co-ordination, in terms of the ability to check out the genitals of a newly hatched chick, becomes masterful. Your hourly numbers increase. Six hundred chicks an hour. Eight hundred chicks an hour. A thousand.

In Seoul, for the poorest of the poor, chick-sexing is a career opportunity. If you're good, you can spend time in European chicken factories, and send money back home – but only if you're good. Only if you're a top, top sexer.

One top sexer had the credentials. They were on their way. A top sexer in the making. Their numbers were good. Many hundreds an hour. But then something happened. The numbers started dropping off. Their hand–eye co-ordination started slipping. Maybe it was drink. Some people thought it was drink. Or a soured relationship. They had been top of the class. They'd actually helped some of the slower ones with their sexing. But it all went wrong.

There was no getting away from it: Their sexing was off. In the end, they didn't make the cut. Didn't get one of the coveted jobs in a factory farm. But three people from their class really lucked out; they got three of the best-paid sexing jobs in the whole of the chicken world – in a factory in the countryside.

Something snapped inside that top sexer's mind. It was all to do with losing face. They believed that the glory should have belonged to them. One of those jobs, in the factory, should have been theirs. As a sexer, they had talent. These other people, they were plodders at best. Why them? The unhappy sexer visited the former classmates. The idea was to break into their houses and then stab them to death. They killed two sexers. And a *kid*, for Christ's sake.

By the way, what happens to the discarded male chicks is this: they grind them up in a grinder. Some they freeze for people to give to their pet snakes. I don't think they kill them first.

I look at the trolley girl. Channelling the younger Belfort. He'd think: she lives in a big, dirty house with plywood walls closing in around small rooms. She wants to send money back home to Vodka-land, but never has enough. Her boyfriend has short sandy hair and a gold tooth. They do coke, ecstasy. He hits her.

I take the money out of my pocket. The girl smiles. If her cheekbones were 5 per cent more prominent, she'd be worth millions. She'd be a Victoria's Secret Angel, a seller of underwear, making millions by persuading the merely adequate that they are inadequate.

As things are, her days are numbered. Soon, there'll be a robot trolley. And robot chick-sexers, and robots chucking the male chicks in the grinders, maybe even robot serial killers. One day soon someone will write a thriller featuring a robot serial killer, and I wish I could say that person might be me.

'And a Mars bar.'

She is hot to the touch as she hands over the hot steaming cup, the toothsome brown ingot. I give her the last of my money and raise the flat of my hand. She keeps the change.

***

Coffee – at last! My heart rattles and clicks just from the smell.

I should really be closing in on Belfort. I need to find the key to him. You can always find the key to someone if you look hard enough. You need to keep going through the facts, to get to the essential person.

How he made the money.

Why he turned to crime.

OK. Let's try to understand him.

Don't judge him – yet.

He's very bright. Always did well at school. His mother was a Tiger Mom. That Chinese thing. Except it exists everywhere. What did you score on your test today, Jordan? Only 90? That's his mother. She wants him to be a doctor, a dentist. Actually pushes him to go to dental school. Which he does. But he drops out after three weeks.

Dropping out feels good.

And … he becomes a salesman. He wants to sell. Instant gratification. It's a drug. Exchanging things for money. Persuading a person to part with money. The persuasion part is the strongest addiction at first.

He's always liked selling. Go back to when he's sixteen; he sells ice creams on the beach. Buys the ice cream in bulk. Jones Beach, Long Island. Something clicks. He makes tens of dollars a day. Then a hundred. Then more. This *works*. He's good. Approaching another human being, working on the angle of approach, getting the angle right, collecting the money, moving on.

The purity of money, the way it annuls all obligations, curtails all relationships, quantifies his powers of persuasion, provides feedback, clears the mind, gives clarity, the *window of clarity* he would later call it, when he could see a sale, could feel a sale, the open and the close of it, the straight line between the open and the close, the target in his cross-hairs, the bullet aimed and fired, the sale closed, the prey killed, all of life now simplified, all anxieties banished, not worried now about not becoming a doctor, or a dentist, or a lawyer like his brother, not worried about his two cousins who went to Harvard, he must have heard that line a million times, ringing around his head, this guy who went to Harvard, that guy who went to Harvard, all of this washed away in one simple act, the act of exchanging things for money, being good at exchanging things for money, and then better, and then great, the sky the limit, the possibilities endless ...

And yes, I'm beginning to get the guy, he's a pure salesman, a salesman to the core, and thinking this, feeling happier, I look at the table in front of me, at the cardboard cup, at my coffee.

I can still taste chocolate, am desperate for more chocolate.

I gulp my coffee.

***

Number one. How does he make the money? He's a stockbroker. A broker of stocks – shares of companies.

He buys the stock. Then he makes people want it by telling them it's going to rise in value.

He *creates demand*. And this demand is what makes the stock rise in value. Demand makes it look different. We all understand this instinctively: demand is value. It's a playground craze. I want it because you want it; I want it more because you have it; give it to me, give it to me now, I'll give you all my sweets! The demand grows as the supply shrinks.

The demand feeds on itself.

Belfort manipulates the market. He's a conjuror of demand, which appears to have magic qualities. He's created a little machine that fuels itself.

But his job is not done – ideally, he wants to advise his clients to sell at the top of the market, to get them out before demand starts to wane. He tries to sense how much a stock will go up before it starts to fall; how a sequence of events, certain things happening in the right order, will dramatically alter the value of a stock, which is an idea about the future profits of a company or a brand, an idea about an idea about an idea.

When people see this idea getting more popular, they are attracted to it, they buy it, so the price keeps on going up, which makes yet more people buy it. Keynes said the stock market is like a beauty contest, but with a subtle difference. It's not about picking the most beautiful girl. It's about guessing who *other people* will see as the most beautiful girl, and picking her.

It's not about being right. It's about being smart.

And if you're smart, you know the price can't keep on rising for ever; at some point, it will start to drop. You need to know *exactly* when to turn back.

At Investors' Center, the crummy office where he works, the culture is to pitch cheap stocks to average Joes – schlumps who have a bit of spare money, but not much.

He starts Stratton. He tries different strategies. He tweaks. He pitches cheap stocks to rich people, and discovers that rich people don't buy cheap stocks. All this time, he's getting better and better at selling, at persuading; he begins to coach other brokers.

The cult is taking shape. People want to follow him. He wants to be their leader. And then he hits on something: a sweet spot in the market. He knows that rich people normally buy blue-chip stocks for hundreds or thousands of dollars a share. But the problem is that it's hard to manipulate stocks at this price level. So he goes one notch up from the cheapest stocks. Will rich people buy at, say, $5 per share?

It turns out they will. They *will*.

This is the moment the penny drops. He's in his office in Lake Success.

He already knows how to build a little machine that seems to fuel itself. But now, if he can get access to more money, real money, he can build a big one. A big money machine.

To do this, all he needs is persuasion. He just needs to explain to rich people that he will make them richer. Because then – then he gets access to their money. With their money, he can build the big self-fuelling machine. Money creates demand, and demand creates more money. It's the alchemy of finance. An idea about an idea about an idea suddenly crystallises, suddenly breaks out, suddenly looks like a good idea, a great idea, and the odds change, and the graph climbs, steep, steeper, and now is the time, don't stop, *now*, do it!

***

What he sees: you can't build the machine for expensive blue-chip stocks. So you need to find the cheapest stocks that rich people will buy. Then the machine comes to life. You need to look for the sweet spot, need to look for something that's not there, until your eyes make it appear, it's a magic trick, an illusion; it's not there, it's not real, and you keep looking, keep believing, and then it's there, and then it's real.

You can see it. Others can't. And this is what makes you rich – the blindness of others.

Now he gets it. How the game works. How the machine works. Money is lascivious and narcissistic. It lusts after itself. Then it replicates. To make money, you have to be a matchmaker. You have to introduce the money to the money. That's why people like to gamble. It's because the money inside them is itching for some action, it's always hungry, like an addict.

Locate the money. Seduce the money. Make it gush.

He has always known about the buried treasure. Now he has the map.

He is not, I'm thinking, a man of principle. His modus operandi is to create an information mirage, making something look better than it actually is. For a while, in any speculative market, making something look better means that it actually is better, because value is all about perception – but only for a while.

He's a beautician. Master of the beauty contest. He knows how to dress up financial products so they look hot. He's like one of those fashion photographers – the Steven Meisel of financial products.

He's twenty-five, twenty-six: he makes $20,000 per month, then $40,000, then $70,000. He's a player, not to mention arrogant, and insolent, and self-absorbed, and materialistic. Does a criminal mentality already lurk in his psyche? It's tempting to think so. But he's not a criminal – not yet, anyway.

***

He's Tom Sawyer.

He's Tom Sawyer whitewashing the fence, in the story by Mark Twain.

In which Tom, a teenage boy, living with his aunt in the antebellum Deep South, does something bad, and the aunt punishes him, tells him he must whitewash her garden fence, which he doesn't want to do, which he hates the idea of doing, because it sounds like hard work, and because doing it will be humiliating; people will walk past and see him humbled, with his bucket and brush. So he whines, but the aunt is unrelenting, and now here he is, feeling low, painting this whitewash on the fence, hating it, and one of his friends spots him, and asks him what he's doing, and Tom, saving face, tells his friend how amazing it is to do this whitewashing, how good it feels.

And the friend asks Tom if he can have a go, and Tom carries on whitewashing, and the friend asks again, and Tom says no, *he* wants to whitewash the fence, he *loves* whitewashing the fence, and then finally Tom allows the other guy to whitewash a tiny strip of fence, but only a tiny strip, after which he must give the brush back … he's quite strict about this … and more boys appear, and they all want to try whitewashing the fence, and finally Tom says yes, if they line up, they can all have a go, *for a fee*, and when the aunt comes to check on Tom, to see how chastened he is, to crow and gloat over his humiliation, she sees him sitting on a chair, smiling, happy, taking money, while the other boys line up to do his job.

And you want to cheer. You want to be Tom. You want to feel like Tom feels. Because Tom has performed a trick; he's changed the world inside someone else's head – and others have followed, and their world has shifted, too, Tom has created something out of nothing, he's a guru, he's the pied piper, people are lining up.

***

And now I see that, for the young Belfort, this is the heart of it, this is the magic, the fact that you can *tell* people that something is valuable, and, if your telling is perfect, they'll believe you, they'll see things in a new light, the thing *will* become more valuable, just because you said it would; this is *illocutionary force*, to use the words of the philosopher J.L. Austin, when words become deeds; you can *create value*, can in fact make yourself valuable, just by speaking words.

You can invent pictures in people's heads, and make them follow you, and soon afterwards others will follow the people who are following you.

You are the leader, and you are pushing the buttons, pulling the levers, creating an emotion that feels like happiness, you are creating a part of the world in your image, and this is the essence of *persuasion*, from the Latin *persuadeo*, which means to make something sweet, to prettify, to charm, which itself means *to cast a spell*, charm being a form of magic, or conjuring ... so when you persuade, you cast a spell by *probing another person's mind*, finding the gap in that mind, the hole, the desire, measuring the need, seeking the pain, everybody has something missing, don't they, everybody hurts.

So you locate the need, the lack, the lacuna, the hole, the poisoned well, and then you persuade, which is an art, it's presenting *the thing you've got*, whatever it is, as *the thing they need*, whatever it is.

It's finding the wound and selling the bandage, the old Don Juan routine, as described in the literature of *pick-up artists*, in which the artist, the trickster, approaches the woman, makes contact in an oblique way, creates intrigue, a mystery; it's about being patient, moving forward in increments, towards compliance, towards consent, always aware of the picture in the other person's head, taking two steps forward and one step back, creating scarcity, probing for the weak spot, stroking the weak spot, offering something and then taking it away.

Circling back and forward. Digging a pipeline to the other person's reservoir of need, of pain, always aware that the other person will want to put up a show of resistance, but also that this resistance can be a ritual.

I don't mean that no means yes, not at all, let me make that clear, it's much more subtle than that, in my work as an interviewer it happens all the time.

Someone will say, this is out of bounds, this is not to be talked about, and you agree, and move on, and circle back, and hover, and then move on again, and you see that, actually, the person *does* want to talk about the taboo subject, *does* want to let you in, wants to open the pipeline, needs to open up.

And the resistance is a ritual, a token, and timing is all, and if you time it exactly right, just so, the person will start to open, and then pop! They will gush, will gush right at you, they will buy what you're selling, buy your ability to listen to their story, to shape their story, to turn the pain and the need into a good shape, a pretty shape.

And it feels great.

In these moments you feel important and loved; the guilt comes later, if at all.

***

He is twenty-eight, twenty-nine. He sees other people's minds as mechanisms. The buttons and the levers. He pushes and pulls. He hires more brokers. He teaches *them* the art of persuasion. Develops a system, which he calls the Straight Line. He buys stock, manipulates the price, and sells stock. He makes tens of millions. Buys a white Ferrari, a Range Rover, an Aston Martin, a yacht, a mansion, another mansion.

He's rich.

But then something starts to go wrong. A kind of madness sets in. He's got all these millions. But somehow, he needs more money. He feels *poor*. Some dark force makes him feel *poor*. So he decides to commit a crime, which he thinks is the perfect crime, but is not the perfect crime, because he gets caught.

Number two. Why does he turn to crime?

There's something I'm missing.

***

We're approaching the bridge, the big viaduct across the valley. On this side are trees and fields. On the other side: the suburbs, the river, the palace, the huge domed cathedral, the glass towers in the shape of vegetables and knives.

I look at the trees and the fields.

There's something I'm missing.

He learns how to make money. He learns the trick. He becomes obsessive. *Then* he feels poor.

One of my editors, Celia, thinks I'm good with obsessive people, thinks I understand them, because I'm obsessive myself.

She's right.

I *am* obsessive.

I smile at myself in the window, and then open my mouth, which would be the act of a crazy person if I thought I was in anyone's line of vision, which, momentarily, I'm not. Anyway, my teeth could be better. The front teeth not bad; the back teeth dark with fillings. I need work, a lot of work; I want all of them, every single tooth, to be white and glossy and sharp and clean.

***

Damn! My concentration is broken. I can only focus, actually focus hard, for a certain length of time, and then everything evaporates, and the thing is, it's fine to take a break, to let your mind wander, as long as you, as long as you what, the thought is gone.

***

Damn, *damn*! I have lost my train of thought, something I *must not* do. My coffee is gone. Outside the window I can see low brick warehouses, corrugated asbestos roofs, small and large vehicles; square miles of hard graft.

***

In front of my eyes, on the table, is my coffee cup, and now I think about coffee, how our relationship with coffee has changed, not because of the coffee itself, but because of the places in which we drink the coffee, the urban spaces with soft chairs, where we can look at people, and be looked at by people, and sit with our laptops, doing some sort of work, or making online bets, which is the same thing, in a way, if you see what I mean.

**

We click past the backs of houses, and blocky office buildings, parks, a stadium, under and over bridges, for two seconds I can see a whole high street laid out below me, the people and cars, and then tracks and bridges, the glass towers tiny in the distance.

**

I've got it! I have grasped the problem of what's wrong with losing your concentration.

It's this: every second you let your mind drift is two or three seconds on the way back. Think of mountaineers who get within touching distance of the summit, but they know they should turn back, because even though they have enough time to get to the top, they don't have enough time to get down again – a few more minutes' climbing and the odds change dramatically. They should turn back, but they keep on going, step after addictive step, exposed on a wall of ice, but tunnelling into the depths of a very personal obsession.

Like when Joe Simpson and Simon Yates climbed Siula Grande, in the Peruvian Andes – up they went, step by tiny step, towards the top, mostly seeing just snow and ice in front of their eyes, sharp and clean, blinding white, nailing their pitons into the ice, moving up by increments, and sometimes looking up and to one side, and seeing the summit, where the final white cusp of ice gives way to sky, and they could have turned back, they had the chance, but they didn't turn back, they kept on going, and they got there!

And at some point, the odds changed dramatically, and they tried to get down, stepping carefully, placing their feet in the cracks, another series of tiny steps, and Simpson slipped, and shot down a wall of ice, and smashed his knee, which meant that he probably wouldn't be able to get down, which meant in turn that if Yates tried to help him, he, Yates, probably wouldn't be able to get down, and as Yates lowered himself towards Simpson, Simpson knew he'd know, from the look in Yates's eyes, whether he would definitely die, or whether he would merely probably die ...

And what got them to this point was obsession. When you decide to climb a mountain, it's not just about you and the mountain. It's about you and the rest of the world you inhabit; you want to come back to that world, having climbed the mountain. But then, when you're on the mountain, something happens. At a certain point it stops being about the world outside.

It's just you and the mountain.

So you become like Joe Simpson. Or Doug Hansen, who got to the summit of Mount Everest but did not get back down. He could have turned back. But he did not turn back. And the odds changed dramatically.

Just as the odds changed for George Mallory. They found Mallory's frozen body somewhere near the top of Everest. Nobody ever found Hansen.

You become like those guys. You forget about everything that's not the mountain. You keep on nailing your pitons into the ice face. You keep on scrambling upwards on the ice. You look to your left, and then to your right, and suddenly there it is, through the clouds – the bit where the final cusp of ice gives way to sky. The summit. And you want to be there. Or rather, you feel you are no longer yourself unless you keep trying to get there. And there's a voice in your head. And it's calling out to you. It's saying: turn back. Turn back, or you will slip, and fall. But you can hardly hear that voice.

At some point, you lose touch with that voice. You lose touch with the rest of the world. It's just you and the mountain. And then ...

And then you slip. By then it's easy to slip. The higher you are on the mountain, the easier it is to slip.

***

It's easy to slip. I once got a cheque in the post; this was years ago, when I was earning – or rather, I suppose a better word would be *getting* – a lot of money, getting a lot of money but hugely in debt. There's a reason for this, to do with the mirage-like qualities of money, which I will try to explain. In any case, getting a lot of money, or even quite a lot of money, *was not* good for me. I wish it had been, but it was not.

I was climbing a mountain of money. And I slipped.

So, this cheque. The amount on the cheque was a little more than the average annual wage for somebody in full-time employment, before tax. It was addressed to me. It had nothing to do with me. It was a glitch. A case of mistaken identity. So I made a couple of calls. And I sent a fax. This was in the days of faxes. I called and faxed. Sorry, I said, but –

No, said the guy. Don't be sorry. *We're* the ones that should be sorry.

The thing is, I said, I think I should –

No, said the guy, you should do nothing. It's our fault. You don't need to do anything.

This was a funny moment. I could have insisted. I could have said, look. But I did not.

I thought: let's just hang on a moment. For once in my life!

And: hey, maybe it *is* my money. People are always telling me I owe *them* money.

And: maybe, just this once, they owe *me*.

And: in any case, let's put it into my account.

And: for safekeeping.

And: if nothing else.

And: while I think about it.

And: while I at least *think* about it.

The money was gone in a shocking amount of time. *Shockingly* quick. Bills paid, nice clothes, decent goods and services. A brief holiday from everyday poverty. I don't mean real poverty, of course I don't. But everybody's everyday life feels like poverty, however rich you are. It's one of our society's darker truths. The holiday lasted maybe forty days. Then the money was gone, with nothing to show for it. I mean, it just gets *sucked* away. When you have money, it feels like a handful of dust, and everything around you acts like a Hoover.

I was having a talk with my accountant. I said: 'What if somebody sent you some money?'

'How do you mean?'

'Well, what if somebody, hypothetically, sent you a cheque?'

'Sent you a cheque?'

'I don't know. But let's say somebody sent you a cheque ... out of the blue.'

'Has this happened to you?'

'I'm saying *if* it happened. If somebody said, look, have this money. And you said, OK then, yes, I'll have it, thanks very much ...'

Anyway, my accountant was livid. I might have committed a criminal act, is what he said.

Then I had a phone call. A woman, investigating 'the missing money'.

She came to see me. Had access to all my accounts. This doesn't look good, Mr Leith, she said. I feel a voice telling me to skip over the next bit. But I am forcing myself not to heed the voice.

I was lucky. I still had the fax I'd sent them. It was just enough. No criminal prosecution. I just had to pay the money back. Plus some interest. Which meant I had to pay more interest on the debts I would now pay back more slowly, plus the penalties on the taxes I would now pay back more slowly.

But it was so easy. So easy to slip. To slip and slide. And that is, I think, partly why I'm frightened of money. It is oily. It oils your path. It's slippery underfoot.

The thing I was going to explain. I got some well-paid work. So I had a lot of money. So I upgraded my life, mostly in the area of services. After a while, being able to have better services changes your outlook – changes *you* – even though you don't see it at the time.

Every day of your life, you avoid some kind of confrontation by buying your way out of it. So you become soft and cowardly. You buy luxury. What you're buying is the privilege of being able to indulge your inner coward without being shamed, which is addictive. Your inner coward, it turns out, is also an abusive bully.

You keep on saying, yes, *OK*, and then you buy yourself out of something. The money just drains away. And then, after a period of being abused, certain things, because you need them to, begin to look fuzzy.

Things like the spirit of the law.

And, at a specific, crucial moment, the letter of the law.

It's like deciding to have two drinks, but then after two drinks you're not the same person who decided to have two drinks. Sort of like that.

Everybody slips in their own way, for their own reasons. It's so *personal*. So *intimate*. So *embarrassing*. And then, eventually, somebody knocks on your door. They sit down. You sit down. You wait for them to say something.

I'm thinking about that moment. The exact emotion of that moment. The knock on the door. The woman. 'The missing money'. There's a few seconds in which cold electricity passes downwards through your body.

The woman came into my house. She wanted to look through my accounts. Her finger moved down the page, her expert eye no doubt computing the hotels, restaurants, the repetitiously large amounts of cash extracted in the early hours, during drug binges.

This woman. Expert finger moving down the columns. Kestrel eyes fixed forward.

She's brusque. I, on the other hand, am all edgy charm, agreeing to everything, offering tea and biscuits, which she does not want, or says she does not want; I'm standing over her, watching the finger as it cruises across the numbers, formulating in my mind the questions that might be asked, the answers that might be given.

You slip, and then you start to cut corners, and you slip some more; you slip, and the bourgeois mask you've been wearing slips; you slip, and you try to make things right, but you can't. It's too late.

Belfort, salesman, discovered the trick of how to make millions, made millions, and then …

Slipped.

***

It's the *gangster problem*, that's exactly what it is, I now see, as described in the essay by the late, at least I assume late, Robert Warshow – he *must* be dead, for a nanosecond I imagine the funeral, people nodding calmly, he was old.

Remember 'The Westerner', that essay he wrote on gangsters and cowboys? An absolute classic, 'The Westerner'. Reading it, you can tell Warshow is more of a cowboy than a gangster. Just look at Gary Cooper, he says. Look at the guys he played. They're marked by a certain type of indolence. They don't own anything, or want anything. You never see them handle money. They are etched against the landscape, does he say that, *etched*?

But they are. They exist in these vast landscapes, sitting up on the horse, taking it all in with a glance. The world of the frontier. The cowboy's life is mostly about a sort of leisure, contemplative, he's at one with something bigger than himself, with the ways of the frontier, with nature – and that, of course, involves the cruelties of nature, the sudden moments when he *does what he has to do*. And the thing is, he's not actually striving for anything more – he's not trying, as Warshow makes clear, to get ahead. He's not trying to get ahead, because he's already there.

Now look at the gangster – the figure that, on some level, replaced the cowboy in the popular imagination. He's not a man of leisure – he's constantly anxious, always fretting, twitchy.

He's a product of the city. The concrete and the glass. The dirt and the people. The tide of people. In and out. Always needing to be somewhere else.

He's on a treadmill, the city is a treadmill, and it's getting faster and faster. He's whacked one guy, and now he must whack another guy *because* he's whacked the first guy. He needs to kill his enemies, and sometimes he needs to kill his friends. He can trust nobody.

The gangster never enjoys himself – or, if he does, it involves bingeing, compulsive debauchery. He gambles. He's a sex maniac. But he doesn't exactly *enjoy* sex. He buys time with prostitutes, because, for this guy, the pleasure exists in the actual spending of money.

The very word *spending* – he ejaculates money. And Warshow doesn't say this, not quite, or maybe he does, but the gangster is a product of money – he lives in a neurotic world that's an allegory of modern finance. The world of what people call *late capitalism* – where you take risks to buy time to get money, and then take more risks to buy more time, because you always need more money.

The more you get, the more you need, because the thing you get is itself a creator of need. In this world, everything seems to be addictive; every solution turns out to be a new problem.

***

I'm thinking of one particular gangster story, the best gangster story I ever read, and *nobody knows about it*, I've never met anybody else who's read it. Other than people I *told* to read it. But it's the gangster problem in a nutshell.

It's based on a series of interviews with a convicted hitman called Joey. The interviewer was a guy called David Fisher.

The whole book concerns the twenty-ninth kill in Joey's career. The title of the book is *Hit #29*.

I found it in a crime bookshop and packed it for a long flight. I was writing an article about a billionaire called David Gilmour. This guy Gilmour – he'd hit upon pretty much the best business model I'd ever heard of, out in Fiji. He'd found an artesian well, an underground lagoon of water, and he'd sunk a pipeline into this lagoon, and, because the water was under pressure, it gushed out of the ground; it *pumped itself*. So all he had to do was arrange for thousands of plastic bottles to pass over the end of this pipeline, and then, after that, the bottles passed through a lid machine, which put lids on the bottles. The lids were blue.

The factory practically ran itself. Just gushing water and a conveyor belt for the bottles, and a lid machine. Beautifully simple! Gilmour had visualised the whole thing. He owned an island out there, in the Fiji archipelago, where he'd built a resort; I was told it was the most exclusive resort in the world.

Well, maybe. But like, Bill Gates had stayed there. And Steve Jobs. And Tom Cruise. You could see any approaching helicopter or boat from miles away, meaning nobody could photograph you, or film you, if you went there. You have to get a plane to Los Angeles, and then another one to New Zealand, and then another, and another – it takes *days*. The planes get smaller and smaller; by the end you're the only passenger.

So there I was on this island. The only guest. Just me and lots of Gilmour's employees. Maybe a hundred – the gardeners, the people who ran the farm, grew the vegetables, picked the fruit, raised the semi-wild pigs that lived in the woods. I stayed in this beach house for about five days; the idea was to sit around drinking Gilmour's water and thinking about how rich it, the water, had made Gilmour. The *shower* in this place. I kept taking showers.

After a while, I got a sense of how rich Gilmour was. Pretty rich. A billionaire. I sat on a garden chair as young men quietly clipped my shrubs and raked any stray leaves from my lawn.

I drank Gilmour's water. I drank a lot of coffee. Every day someone would come round and consult me about what I wanted to eat, where I wanted to eat it, how I would like it prepared. If you were sneaky, you could try to work out who stayed with Tom Cruise in the days after he announced his divorce from Nicole Kidman, and what they'd done, by reading all the comments in the various guest books.

***

So I started to read this gangster story.

And I could see, right there, how I could make a fortune. Nobody had heard of this book. But in the right hands, it would make a perfect movie.

All I have to do, I thought, is buy the rights, which will be cheap, a few thousand, not much anyway – and then get the right director to read the book, maybe someone who is at the point in their career where they need a surefire hit.

I'd interviewed Francis Ford Coppola, the *Godfather* guy, the *Apocalypse Now* guy, and *he* was pretty desperate. He'd got to the point, he said, where he was reading John Grisham, and underlining what he saw as the key passages, trying to work out what made Grisham such a good storyteller. But you should see his house – Coppola's, that is. I've never seen Grisham's. Coppola's house is *so* impressive. It's in the Napa Valley, at the foot of a hill. It has one of those porches that goes all the way round.

Anyway, he adapted this Grisham book, and made a film of it. It was sort of OK. But not great. Maybe I could try him, I thought.

Or maybe Scorsese, I also thought; I'd interviewed *him* at the time of his weird film *Kundun*, and he seemed a bit lost, too – I couldn't quite see what he was getting at with that film. He sat there, quick nervous talk, and the one thing that stood out was when he said he knew what a great story looked like, could see it immediately, the whole thing was about building intensity, the intensity snowballing until it becomes – this is how I remember it – a sort of monster. Maybe I could try *him*, I thought.

Because this story – oh, it was good. Sitting in this beach house, on my own, had stirred up feelings of grandiosity in me – which, incidentally, always happens to me in these places, these resorts and retreats, always lodgings I could not afford myself, which makes me feel poor and unworthy, but also fiercely aspirational. I sit in loungers, alone and highly caffeinated, making notes for screenplays and thrillers I never write.

Damn, I'm thinking, damn! I missed the boat with Scorsese; he pulled himself out of his bad patch, with *The Departed*, a story about the rivalry between a mobster posing as a cop and a cop posing as a mobster, like two sides of the same brain, hunting each other down in a hall of mirrors ... and, of course, double damn, because now Scorsese is making a film about Belfort; as soon as I saw Belfort's story, even just the blurb, I thought, there's a Scorsese film, it's *exactly* right for him. I'm always missing the boat with these things, is what I'm thinking, a thought I must edit, and quickly. You should never let yourself be haunted by past failures; even I know that.

***

So this guy, Joey, right at the start, he tells us about his twenty-eighth hit. It's perfect. Every step is worked out in advance. He's researched the guy he's going to kill. He's entered the guy's mindset. He knows where the guy goes, how the guy thinks.

The guy is in a restaurant in Brooklyn. It's 1968. An era of big cars. The age of Motown. Sinatra still at his height. Mobsters still wearing suits. You can just see it. Can't you just see it? Night time. Joey walks into the restaurant, goes into the men's room, checks his gun, checks his spare gun, locks and loads, comes out of the men's room, gun in hand, if it was a movie the camera's eye would now be looking at the restaurant from across the street, it would look like a Hopper painting, the shadows and dim lights, and you'd hear the three shots, the screams of the diners, and then you'd see Joey opening the door and walking through the door, and then maybe a freeze-frame on Joey as the door swings back.

And then you could have a voiceover: 'That's me, just after my twenty-eighth hit. Everything worked out fine. It was perfect. I'm twenty thousand dollars richer than I was half a minute ago. The only problem was that twenty thousand. Because what I really needed, at that moment in time, was forty thousand.'

He needs to kill again. For the twenty-ninth time.

And *now* we've got a movie.

In the book, Joey tells us about his life – in other words, about the gangster problem. He kills people, and he also works as a debt collector in the illegal gambling industry. He's a sort of enforcer. But he's laconic. He's wry. You like him.

You get to see that this guy is successful because people respect him, and they respect him because they know he's prepared to kill.

So if he doesn't keep killing, at some point he's finished.

Which makes him stressed.

So he needs an escape. So he gambles. He has a gambling problem. And the women – he has a wife and a girlfriend. He throws money at them. The release of spending. The ejaculation of money. It's a nightmare – in order to ejaculate, in other words to de-stress, he needs to keep killing people, which of course stresses him out more, which makes him need to ejaculate more, on and on, a vicious circle.

He's a workaholic.

He's at the point of burnout.

But he can't stop.

And then he takes a mis-step. He slips. Up until now, he's been meticulous about the work he does. But now he's desperate. He needs that extra twenty thousand. So he takes on a job he's not *quite* sure about. The job is to kill a guy called Joe Squillante.

And the thing about this Joe Squillante is … *he's just like Joey*. Same age. Same job. Same *name*. Like Joey, Squillante's a mobster. Like Joey, he's a debt collector in the illegal gambling industry. Like Joey, he's got a terrible gambling problem. Like Joey, he's in a deep financial hole. So he's been stealing money from the mob. He's crossed a line.

Like Joey, Squillante is a workaholic.

Like Joey, he's at the point of burnout.

And now Joey must get inside his head …

You see? It's another hall of mirrors. It's a maze – a psychological maze. It's a study of paranoia. In the right hands – a classic. It's all about what happens when you can't see the big picture any more, when you're not the guy on the horse taking in the view, but the guy on the treadmill, going nowhere, tunnelling into the closed world of your own mind.

***

And for a moment, here in the dark carriage, I visualise my coup. Buying the rights to the book. Leveraging the value of the rights. Talking on the phone. The alchemy of turning maybe into yes. Yes! And then the inevitable aftermath – the wealthy version of myself.

The things I could have! The new house, long and low, modern and brutal, behind a screen of topiary. Uncluttered rooms like galleries. Works of art like bodily fluids splashed on the walls.

The porn mansion, I'm thinking.

It's always either the porn mansion or the country pile. Personally I could never make up my mind – until recently. Walking along a quiet street about a mile from where I live, I saw the perfect porn mansion – long and low, insolent and beautiful, early 1960s. It's where the bad guy would live in a 1970s movie. It's the bad guy house.

Perfect, I thought, perfectly tucked, tucked so neatly into the landscape. I *want* it, I thought, want to get *inside* it, want it to be *mine*. No way a country pile could compete, I thought. Now I've made up my mind, I thought.

Belfort, of course, didn't have to, because he had both. The big house in Old Brookville, a redbrick compound, with outbuildings, resident servants, an ornamental pond, gravel drive, gardeners clipping the hedges. That's the country pile. And then the beach house in the Hamptons: white, gleaming, translucent and balconied. Seething with money and idealised women – the porn mansion.

He wanted both. Just like he wanted the Ferrari *and* the Range Rover *and* the Aston Martin *and* the Mercedes *and* the limousine, *and* the chauffeur to drive him around *and* the yacht *and* the helicopter *and* the private jets; nobody can be in two places at once, but there comes a moment when you at least have to *try* – and this, I now see, is when everything begins to unravel, it is a specific sort of madness.

You cross a line. You keep on going.

He wanted it all. He wanted to have his cake *and* eat it. Wanted to own the stocks *and* sell them, wanted to do the cocaine *and* the Quaalude tranquillisers, wanted to have sex with his wife *and* the Miller Lite model, and then when the Miller Lite model was his wife, he wanted to have sex with her *and* the prostitutes, the sex brokers, I must ask him about this, about his dick, why wasn't it, why didn't it … but not until the interview has settled down, nothing about his penis, or the prostitutes, or even the drugs, until later, when trust has been built.

I'm closing in on him. He climbed. Took one step too many. The odds changed. Then he fell.

Committed the crime and sank the yacht and crashed the Merc and lost the wife and the family and the houses and the money, went to jail and now he's out, on condition that he pays back what he owes, which is $100 million.

I'm closing in on him.

But fuck! Now I've got this far, I can see I'm going to be late.

What is wrong with me? What is *wrong*?

The train is crawling into a station.

It's not my station.

It's the station before my station.

By now, I should have got off at my station, should have been on the previous train, should have responded to my first alarm clock, gone to bed earlier, lived my life differently, according to different principles.

What is *wrong*?

My stomach is cold.

Why not just jump out at this station? If I could jump out, if I could grab a cab, if I ran into the street and grabbed a cab … there must be a problem with this idea, I'm sure there's a problem, there must be.

There is a problem, there *is*, but I can't quite pin it down, can't think of it.

The problem.

What *is* it?

My hands are touching my pockets, checking my recording device and my spare recording device. My shoulder is braced against the strap of my man-bag. I am possessed by a powerful, liberating urge to jump. To jump, and then to run, to run and keep running, I am itching for movement.

The doors slide open.

2

The doors slide open.

I step out, between the sliding doors, and then, thirty-three minutes later, I step into the lobby of the Chelsea Harbour Hotel, between the sliding doors, into the hushed world of money.

The hushed world, where you are treated as if you are rich. Because, after all, if you are here – and if you don't bear any striking signs of dysfunction – there is at least some chance you might be rich.

I said earlier that I write about rich people. But nobody ever asks me to write about poor people. OK, there were the Koreans I knelt down with that time. They were pretty poor. They had a small house, very neat and tidy. They might have tidied it up when they knew I was coming. But I actually think they were tidy by nature. But, anyway, there were those Koreans, and another time there were some people in Mexico in a shanty town, which was my subject – the shanty town, not these particular people. My subject was overpopulation, the idea of there being too many people in one place, in this case because something had sucked them, all these people, to this place, had made them leave their farms, their crops, their horses, their way of life, to come to the city, to get ahead, but it hadn't worked, had it?

Sometimes, in the old days, a Sunday magazine would want a story about poverty.

Not so much now.

What I said, in this particular story, was that as you travelled out from the city, as you made progress through the shanty town, you could tell where you were in terms of depth of poverty. After a few miles, I said, all the words disappeared, there were no street signs – because, beyond a certain point, people are illiterate. That was the gist of it, anyway. They'd built all these shacks, well-organised, in rows, like garden sheds or beach huts.

When I got out of the car, the people I could see ducked back into the shacks, and I stood there, took a few pictures of the shacks, and got back in the car.

Picturesque poverty – an invention of the 1970s, I think, in magazines at least. Used in exactly the right way, it makes the reader respond well to the ads. Pictures of open-cast mines, pinched faces, mean dwellings, smiling people with missing teeth and fingers, photogenic women who don't know they're photogenic, enormous rubbish heaps ... and then when you look closely you can see how small the people are who are climbing them, mountaineers of rubbish. Readers would look at these pictures and feel obscurely invigorated, and maybe they'd want to upgrade their outdoor furniture.

But as I step, damp and despicable, into the hushed world, I'm not thinking about the Koreans kneeling in their small, neat house, or the Mexicans ducking into their shacks.

I am thinking about the rich. If you wanted to take a snapshot of my attitude to the rich, this exact moment would be the perfect time.

My front foot is activating the ultrasonic sensor. My eyes are scanning the glass panels. The slit between the panels widens. My own reflection disappears from my field of vision, giving way to the moneyed space beyond.

A snapshot of my mind, at this exact moment. I am thinking about money, about wealth, about *the rich*. A tiny proportion of the world's population, but the vast majority of the people I write about.

I write about the super-rich and the very rich. Sometimes just the rich. From the Latin *rex*, meaning ruler, he who regulates. But as the word moved through the centuries – *rix* in middle French, and then the modern French *riche*, the Spanish *rico*, the English *rich* – it, the word itself, took on new wealth, new status. It used to mean the regulator – the man in charge, the monarch (from the ancient Greek *arche*, meaning first, in other words the guy who was there from the beginning, the guy who was a local god, a small-town divine, which is why the Latin for rich is *dives*). In the old days it was all about getting there first, staking a claim, building a castle, making rules, and telling people that these rules are a description of the natural order.

But then the idea of richness took on a new tone. Rich started to mean fertile, productive, fecund. A focal point of growth and ferment. Rich soil turns the seed into the harvest; the *costa rica* gives you tons of raw sugar in exchange for a small number of slaves. A rich place is a site of exploitation, of mastery, of progress.

We think being rich means having stuff, that it's a state of having, and that's true, up to a point. But it's also about the magic of begetting. It's about replication.

It's sexual.

***

Walking across the threshold, between the glass panels, eyes peeled, scanning for Belfort, my mind alights on another moment, a year or so earlier, when I stepped into Dorsington, the Warwickshire estate of the tycoon Felix Dennis, who had made £500 million in the world of glossy magazines. He had sensed the vast roiling energy that was the world's desire for gadgets, and found a way to harness it. He created an international empire of gadget magazines, and then expanded into softcore – pictures of young women, mostly in their early twenties, sometimes younger, not fully dressed. But his first big idea, the flash of genius that set him on his way, had been a poster of Bruce Lee that you could fold like a map.

Dorsington! For a while, travelling along a quiet road, I'd wondered exactly where the countryside ended and Dorsington began. I went past a tiny village, somewhere near the birthplace of William Shakespeare. There were no road signs. The ancient houses had thatched roofs. Someone had recently replaced and trimmed the thatch on all the houses at the same time, which was, I thought, unusual. The hedges were too neat to be real hedges. But they were real hedges. There were bushes, and animals in the bushes. But the animals were not real animals. They were bronze statues of animals.

I got out of the car and walked towards a barn that was not a barn; even from a distance, I could tell it was not an actual barn.

Where was Dennis?

As I walked towards the barn that was not a barn, I was thinking of another day, a couple of years previously, when I climbed the stairs of a blocky office building in outer London, looking for the tycoon Alan Sugar. Sugar had made £700 million selling hi-fi equipment and personal computers. He had a knack for making cheap things look like their more expensive rivals in the market.

Sugar's building appeared to be empty, even though it was a weekday morning. His beige Mercedes was one of two cars in the car park. I'd been told Sugar was definitely somewhere in the building. I ducked into the staff bathroom, where I had a nosebleed. I screwed a paper towel into a tight cone, and spiralised it into the nostril that was bleeding. I ran the tap and washed the blood out of the basin. My memory tells me I checked myself out in the mirror. My breath, which smelled of alcohol from the night before, created a circle of mist that obscured my face.

Sugar had had an idea in the 1960s when he saw the clear plastic lid of a butter dish at his mother-in-law's house. He looked at the lid, and then he had the idea, and the idea was worth millions. The lid was like a small version of the dust cover on a hi-fi turntable, but *so* much cheaper to make than those currently on the market. Sugar's company grew and grew, expanding into bigger and bigger buildings, including the one I was in.

In Sugar's bathroom I washed the caked blood off my chin and thought of another day, when I'd walked along the top floor of one of the two towers of the Westin Hotel in Seattle looking for the tycoon Howard Schultz. He was supposedly in the Presidential Suite. He was expecting me. The hotel overlooked Puget Sound, just along from the harbour-front spot where Kurt Cobain had told a documentary maker that money definitely does not make you happy. *He* suffered from what I think of as Kurt Cobain syndrome, a specific type of depression that happens to very successful people.

Anyway, Schultz had made perhaps a billion dollars after he invented the coffee chain Starbucks. I'd just watched him give a talk to an arena full of Starbucks employees. Every plastic chair in the arena had a dollar bill stuck underneath it, right below where you were sitting.

The talk had been very like a talk I'd attended by the motivational speaker Tony Robbins. Schultz even looked like Robbins. He said he had learned something important. It was: 'Take the moment! Seize it!'

In my memory he told everybody to reach underneath their seats. Everybody did.

Schultz had his big idea when he went to Italy and stepped into a cafe. The idea had not just been about coffee. It was about attracting people in cities to comfortable places where they would spend money. The most productive use of urban real estate. Schultz says he grasped it immediately – a flash of inspiration. Then he took. Then he seized.

I was in the Westin's upper lobby, a cube of silver, tan and white, my mind racing through images of other tycoons I had in some way pursued – Steve Wynn, for instance, who had made hundreds of millions in the casino business. I was thinking of Wynn, and of Ingvar Kamprad, the boss of Ikea, and Sol Kerzner, the South African casino chief, and Flavio Briatore, the Benetton boss, and I was thinking of Wynn's collection of Old Masters in Las Vegas, his Gauguin and his Van Gogh, his Pollock and his Picasso, and I was thinking of Kamprad's yellow guest house at the edge of Kamprad's lake in Kamprad's Swedish forest, Briatore's college-like campus in north-east Italy, Kerzner's little island in the Bahamas. At this point I had yet to visit Gilmour's island. Gilmour's was actually a better island. Kerzner's was scrubby. Nice enough but scrubby. It's actually quite hard to stop a tropical island from looking scrubby.

A lot of these guys want to have islands.

Maybe we all want to have a *metaphorical* island. But these guys want a *literal* island. Or a campus, or a compound, or an estate, or a corporation, or a cult. And then, when that happens, when they do become king of the island or the cult or whatever, they sort of change. Just like Henry VII must have changed when he got hold of the throne of England in 1485. Before he got that throne, he would have been thinking: 'Just wait until I get that throne!' Afterwards, he would have sat on that throne, feeling bitter. That's pretty much how Kurt Cobain syndrome works.

I knocked on the door of the Presidential. Schultz answered and I stepped in. Opening the door, I had a sense of melancholy, which might have been to do with what I was going through at the time. I was in Seattle with a girlfriend; the relationship was faltering; I was starting to drink too much. It had been more than eleven years since the execution of Ted Bundy, Seattle's most notorious serial killer, but for some reason I'd thought the tenth anniversary was imminent. I'd missed it by a *whole year*. I walked past a couple of places where he'd abducted people, which really creeped me out.

Bundy had grown up poor. At college he had been engaged to Stephanie Brooks, a beautiful rich girl, but he didn't fit in with her family, didn't measure up. He lacked class. Stephanie dumped him. Then he worked for years trying to better himself. He got a job in public relations and a place at law school. He called Stephanie again. This time she accepted him. But something went terribly wrong, and they split up for a second time. One story is that he dumped her to get revenge for dumping *him* when he was poor. But I think it's more murky than that. I think *he himself* felt he didn't measure up. I think he suddenly saw that, even if he became a successful lawyer, even if he made money, and even if her family came to accept him, he'd still feel inadequate, still the poor boy – low self-esteem ran through him like a deep fissure.

So they split up. That's when he became obsessed with abducting and killing beautiful women. Beautiful women made him hate himself. He killed at least thirty-five.

On the day before his execution Bundy declared himself a victim of glossy magazines. Sexualised pictures of women – they were getting everywhere. Women as objects. He couldn't help himself. The danger, he said, came from 'magazine racks'.

When you look at the women in those magazines, he said, a 'crack' appears in your psyche. Bundy could, only just, talk about the fact that there *was* a crack in his psyche. But he couldn't talk about what was *in* the crack.

Looking into the crack, he said, would be 'too painful'.

Like Bundy, Howard Schultz had been poor. He grew up in the Bayview housing projects in Canarsie, Brooklyn. In his autobiography, *Pour Your Heart Into It*, Schultz tells a story about dating a girl who introduced him to her father. The father asked Schultz where he was from. Brooklyn, he said. Where in Brooklyn, wondered the father. Canarsie, he said. Where in Canarsie, wondered the father. Bayview Projects, he said.

'Oh,' said the father.

Schultz never forgot that 'Oh'.

In the grip of his obsession, Bundy abducted and killed beautiful women – sometimes two in a single day. Schultz went in a different direction. He too was gripped by an obsession – to open coffee shops. Sometimes he would open two in a single day. He was an insatiable predator of coffee, killing rival coffee shops in towns and cities across the Western world.

The Presidential was bounded by a huge curved window. Schultz was sitting on a big sofa, eating curly fries. There was a blanket of mist lying across Puget Sound, and the mist softened the light from the Pacific sun, and the soft light filled the room in a way that temporarily lifted my spirits.

I was thinking about Howard Schultz as I looked in the mirror of Alan Sugar's bathroom, and I was thinking about Alan Sugar as I walked towards the barn that was not a barn, looking for Felix Dennis. These guys – they were *driven*. So driven they could look at a butter dish, or the inside of an espresso bar, or a picture of Bruce Lee, and see vast quantities of money. But there was something about them I definitely didn't envy.

It might, I thought, be because when I look at a butter dish, I want to see a butter dish.

Where was Dennis, anyway? If you want to know the truth, I feared for his sanity. For one thing, he had recently told a journalist that, some years before, he'd killed a man by pushing him off a cliff. Then he'd said he hadn't, but had merely *thought* he had – his story was that the medication he was taking, mixed with alcohol, had turned him delusional. Somehow, he'd had a vision of murder, and the vision had seemed real. That was his story.

But then, if you believed you'd killed somebody, why tell a journalist? Because, actually, that's what a certain type of killer yearns to do. He wants to kill – but, more importantly, he wants people to know he has killed. He wants to kill *openly* – like Ronnie Kray.

For Ronnie Kray, killing openly was pretty much the main thing in life. He believed you weren't a proper gangster unless you could kill someone in front of witnesses, knowing that nobody would testify against you in court because they were too frightened. Kray didn't just want to kill – he wanted everybody to know he was a killer. That second part was the most important. It was a form of currency. It was almost like money. That's why he wanted his brother, Reg, to kill Jack 'The Hat' McVitie; it was a way for the Krays to print more money. Ron kept nagging Reg to kill. Reg didn't really want to, but he did, in the end – a horrible scene in a kitchen.

The truth about Dennis, I thought, was that he hadn't killed anybody, but he wanted people to think he had, and this desire had slipped out when he was drunk – *in vino veritas*, in a complicated way, because of course it was a case of *in vino mendacium*, the *veritas* being the *mendacium*.

The truth is the lie.

***

I walked into the barn that was not a barn. It was Highfield, Dennis's themed health spa – a half-billionaire's bathroom suite. The underlying theme was *Treasure Island*. Dennis had created a health spa based on the book he had loved as a boy. There were two huge wooden sculptures, one of Robert Louis Stevenson, the book's author, and one of Long John Silver, the main pirate. There was an aquarium full of tropical fish, a swimming pool, jacuzzis, showers, steam rooms. There were indoor palm trees. There were masts with rigging, and crows' nests at the top of the masts. You could climb up to the crows' nests and look down at the pool and the jacuzzis.

Treasure Island is about a teenage boy called Jim Hawkins. When Jim's father dies, he runs away to sea in search of buried treasure. During the course of the story, Jim learns a lot. One of the biggest things is that, at heart, everybody is interested in buried treasure. If you show anybody a map of a faraway island with buried treasure, they will drop everything and try to get to that island. On the way, they will lie, cheat, and kill each other. Importantly, when they get to the island, the treasure will be there. They will find it. They will be rich.

What did Stevenson want to tell us about the human condition? That, at heart, everybody is a pirate, even if most people spend their lives thinking they are anything but. Also, that being a pirate is not the worst thing in the world. But the big lesson is: you'll have more fun hunting for treasure than you will after you actually find it. Being rich is OK. But *getting* rich – that's the thing.

I walked around the pool area. Set into the bottom of the pool was a mosaic of a shipwreck, made from thousands of tiny glass tiles. There was also a mosaic of a treasure chest, full of glittering gold and jewels, an effect created by using fibre-optic cables. From certain angles, the treasure chest appeared to be three-dimensional. A reference to Davy Jones's Locker, the bottom of the sea, the place where pirates go when they die; the expression often used to conjure the spirit of death itself.

Above the pool was a gallery with a life-size wooden sculpture of John Harrison sitting at his desk. Harrison was the clockmaker who designed a formula accurate enough to calculate longitude, which meant that ships setting out in search of treasure would, in future, be more likely to find it.

It took him forty years to design the formula. Then he got it right.

I left Highfield and walked on. There's a lot about Highfield I haven't told you. For instance, there was a miniature cinema in the art deco style of the 1930s, with the addition of huge squashy leather seats designed to hug the body for maximum comfort. There was a garage for Dennis's Rolls-Royce, equipped with a rotating floor, so the driver could be pointing forwards when both entering and exiting. There was a small medieval banqueting hall. There was a study full of rare books. There was a bedroom with a four-poster bed, flanked by full-size wooden sculptures of male and female historical figures. On my way out, a female attendant gave me a book of photographs of Highfield. Dennis, she said, might be further along the road, in a building called the Welshman's, where he sometimes went to think and write poetry.

Dennis had gone off the rails for a while – about ten years – and then he'd decided to become a poet. So he needed to build himself the perfect place in which to write poetry. In fact, he created several perfect writing environments for himself – on his estates in the Caribbean and Connecticut, and also in Manhattan and central London.

He'd slipped, and got himself into a terrible mess. Being a poet was part of his recovery.

When you have an unlimited budget, going off the rails can be a very serious matter, because it takes a rich person longer to reach the place known as 'rock bottom'. The rich person, however wasted he gets, always has a chauffeur-driven car, or fleet of cars, to swish him away. He always has a clean and luxurious room waiting for him at night. He has houses in several different countries. He can rent private jets. He can stay in the Penthouse Suite, or the Presidential Suite, or the Royal Suite, of any hotel he likes. Dennis was a crack addict for six or seven years, during which time he travelled the world, relentlessly partying in the company of expensive sex workers. He fell deeper and deeper into a ravine of mental torment and physical decline.

Then he quit the crack and the escorts, and started to write poetry – a lot of it in the Welshman's.

As I approached the Welshman's, I was thinking about all of this – the drugs, the escorts, the poetry. Dennis had almost died, and maybe he had died spiritually, and he was full of regret, he had a reservoir of regret, and now he was trying to draw on that reservoir to fuel his recovery, by turning it into poetry. An unusual business model. But it seemed to be working – or at least had been working, until the arrival of the vision that he'd pushed a man over a cliff. I had a suspicion that the man he'd killed, perhaps in a spiritual sense, had been himself.

I entered the Welshman's garden – or, to use its official name, 'the Garden of Heroes and Villains'. Up the hill that leads to the Welshman's is an avenue of maybe twenty bronze statues. Later, Dennis would tell me that the market for full-size bronze statues was very limited: just him and a few dictators. It reminded me of the avenue of trees that led to the Greek-looking folly on Kerzner's island. Avenues! There must come a point in a very rich person's life when the rich person realises he can afford an avenue, and that's that – he wants an avenue.

This avenue – it was a really good one. But was it as good as Francis Ford Coppola's avenue of trees in the Napa Valley, Sol Kerzner's avenue in the Bahamas, or the lantern-hung avenue in front of Steve Wynn's Bellagio hotel in Las Vegas?

Yes, it was.

They're very vaginal, these avenues, if you think about it. You have a line of approach, bordered with neat bushes or trees, leading to the entrance, beyond which, hidden, lies the main attraction. Just before you arrive, there's often a water feature. Coppola and Wynn had water features. Wynn even staged shows using fountains, when he'd turn on the water jets, and set the whole thing to music, maybe a Michael Jackson song or something by the Bee Gees, which sounds crass, but if you actually see it, with the lighting and the music, and the way he gets the water to jet about in different directions ... it's still crass, but somehow it doesn't *seem* so crass, because of Wynn's confidence.

The confidence of these people!

I'd recently read a story about Wynn. He'd bought a Picasso called *Le Rêve*. It's a 1932 painting of Picasso's girlfriend at the time, Marie-Therese Walter. In the painting, Walter's head appears to be split into two parts. Anyway, Wynn agreed to sell *Le Rêve* to the hedge-fund billionaire Steve Cohen for $139 million. But just before the sale went through, he accidentally elbowed the canvas, puncturing Walter's thigh. Wynn put the sale on hold while the painting was restored. In the end, Cohen bought it a year later for $155 million; in the time it took to mend the painting, the market for Picasso had risen.

People didn't exactly think *Le Rêve* had become more beautiful during the course of 2006. But on some level they thought others would think it had. Anyway, Wynn actually made money by damaging the painting. By doing something really clumsy, which took him one second, he made as much money as an average American would make in eight lifetimes.

I walked up the avenue towards the Welshman's. Every few feet, on either side of me, was a bronze statue. They cost hundreds of thousands, these statues. They take months to make. Looking at them was like looking into Dennis's psyche during his crack period, when he'd commissioned a lot of them.

The statues: Chuck Berry, doing the famous 'duck walk'. The young Bob Dylan strumming his guitar while the much older Woody Guthrie lies in his hospital bed, close to death. Stephen Hawking in his motorised wheelchair. The young Charles Darwin riding a giant Galapagos turtle. Einstein frying an egg. Galileo in old age, blindly fingering a globe. The cartoonist Robert Crumb. The fictional sailors Jack Aubrey and Stephen Maturin. Van Gogh in the act of painting. The thing he's painting – a chair. Muhammad Ali, gloved hands above his head. Bruce Lee performing a kung-fu kick.

I was trying to get a sense of Dennis, of who he was, who he had been. A fatherless boy, small for his age, bullied at school, disliked by teachers, mouthy and toxic. Later, a bearded hippie, furiously ambitious, who one day spotted a long line of young men. He checked them out. They were misfits, damaged creatures, little guys, losers. On one level, he knew all about them – who they were inside, how they felt. He looked up, and saw where they were going. They were waiting in line to buy tickets for a martial arts film. The star of the film was Bruce Lee.

The bearded hippie saw the line of losers. Or maybe he didn't see the line of losers. Maybe he had already passed through the looking glass.

Maybe he just saw the money.

And then he really took off. He had seen Bruce Lee posters in arty shops. But he sensed, the money in him sensed, that maybe 99 per cent of Bruce Lee fans did not go into arty shops. But surely they bought comics and magazines – so why not create a Bruce Lee poster, and then fold it up? It would look like a magazine. You could put it on a rack, next to the magazines and comics. On the back of the poster, you could print factoids about Bruce Lee. You could advertise other Bruce Lee products!

The money inside Felix Dennis saw something – something people would want. He saw beauty through the eyes of others. He would just need to explain it to the right people.

He made calls. He negotiated. Made offers and deals. And … yes! He raked in thousands, tens of thousands. Next, he wondered if George Lucas, who had just made a sci-fi film, a sort of Western set in space, wanted someone to create and distribute fan merchandise. He did. Again – yes! Dennis made millions. Next, he noticed that the world was developing an appetite for digital gadgets – PCs and laptops and palm pilots. Did the companies who made these things want an environment in which to advertise them? They did. Dennis launched a slew of computer magazines. Yes, yes, yes! He made tens of millions. He said he had one talent: 'I see what people will want five minutes before they see it themselves.' A very lucrative talent. He made hundreds of millions. At some point, he saw that he couldn't help himself. At some point, he died a spiritual death. At some point, he became a crack addict. At some point, he fell into a ravine of self-hatred and torment.

The water feature at the top of the avenue was a circular pond. A shiny pool. Suspended above the pool, in an attitude of falling – falling to his death – was a bronze statue of Icarus, the character from Greek mythology whose wings melted when he flew too close to the sun.

Beautiful! Head first, legs akimbo, a look of horror on his face. In the blink of an eye, he will be dead. Less than the blink of an eye – he has blinked for the last time. His eyes are open. He'd been told his wings would melt. He *knew* his wings would melt. But he flew too close to the sun – why? Because he couldn't help himself. A sort of madness. He'd left the Earth behind. It was just him and the sky. Until …

I opened the door of the Welshman's, looking for Dennis, and there he was.

***

A snapshot of my mind, as I walk through the automatic door of the Chelsea Harbour Hotel. I am thinking about the rich. All my ideas and experiences are packaged into a powerful emotion – a powerfully negative emotion. The rich, it tells me, are sad and delusional – and so is the part of me that yearns to be rich.

Sad and delusional!

The statues and islands, the vaginal avenues and phallic towers, the shiny cars, the fat tyres, the trophy wives, the hot women and cool pools, the plunge pools and reflecting pools, the hidden pools and infinity pools, I *love* these pools, but …

Sad and delusional!

So sad, so sad … I'm thinking of Kurt Cobain, of the gun, of turning the gun towards his temple, closing the close-set eyes on his nevertheless handsome face, and squeezing the trigger; and of Reg Kray, who I saw, once, in the pallid and wasted flesh, unfolding himself from a car, at his brother Charlie's funeral, his hands shackled because of that horrible moment in the kitchen; and of Wynn, and of Wynn's elbow, and of Kerzner, of the dreadful helicopter accident in which he lost his son – the rich die in helicopters I'm thinking, helicopters and private jets – and I'm also thinking of Sugar, who told me he is happiest in a tiny plane, in the clouds, away from everybody else, he studied for his pilot's licence, took the test and passed, and now hops over to France, Le Touquet he said, for tea, and then hops back, you meet nice people he said, the hobby pilots who fly the small planes; and

I'm thinking of Belfort, how *he* almost died in a helicopter crash, and of how he had a moral crash, a spiritual crash, an addiction crash, a domestic crash, when he pushed his wife down the stairs, and he took their daughter, who was a toddler, and put her in the car, and tried to drive her away, the wife screaming in the drive, in front of the carport, the former Miller Lite girl, the beautiful model, blonde and sharply pretty with long legs, this beautiful woman screaming in the drive and I'm thinking of Belfort, out of control, his daughter not strapped in properly, smashing the car into the fancy gate at the end of his fancy driveway, and in that moment – bang! – he must have seen himself, seen what he had become.

And I'm thinking of Icarus, eyes open, frozen in bronze a foot above the circular pond next to the Welshman's.

In the Welshman's, Dennis told me this: 'You cannot be seeking yourself when you're making money, because the very process of making money ensures you will create a false identity, a carapace, with which to deflect the many rocks and bullets that will be aimed at you.'

He paused for a moment. 'And if you don't create that carapace, then you will rapidly fall off a cliff, which I just about did anyway. So the very making of money is, in the end, a miserable business.'

A snapshot of my mind. A miserable business I'm thinking. Falling off a cliff I'm thinking. Rock bottom I'm thinking. A long way down I'm thinking, as the slit between the panels widens, as my own reflection disappears from my field of vision, giving way to the moneyed space beyond.

***

Five minutes later, I'm sitting at a table in the bar of the Chelsea Harbour Hotel. On the other side of the table is Jordan Belfort. He's wearing a striped shirt, new jeans and crisp white trainers.

Belfort is saying: 'Here's the thing I believe more than anything – there's only one way to get rich, and that's quick. You have to get rich quick.'

He pauses. For about one second. Then he says: 'That's not through a get-rich-quick *scheme.*'

To our left is the harbour, with its bobbing pleasure boats. To our right is the long curved bar.

He says, 'You always get rich quickly. There's just a lot of work that has to happen before you get yourself in a *position* to get rich. In other words, you always get rich quick. The hardest I ever worked in my life is when I was making no money. When you're doing really well, the money pours in quickly.'

A light goes on and off inside my head.

Belfort says: 'You have to get the pieces of the puzzle into place. But when you've got 'em – bam! You get rich quick.'

He talks in the style of someone who knows what he's talking about. He does not compute as someone who is $100,000,000 in debt.

My brain is making calculations.

Like: if he paid back 99 per cent of what he owes, his debts would still add up to more money than I've ever had.

And: if I made 1 per cent of what he owes, I'd be able to pay off all my debts, including my mortgage, and then I could … and at this point, my mind is full of the bright white happiness I associate with spending money; I can see clean surfaces, a potent shower head, a fresh start in a place where everything fits.

Belfort says: 'There were four things I did, at the highest level, that caused me to soar financially. And there were two things I did at the highest level, bad things, which caused me to crash and burn. Four good, two bad. You avoid these two things, do these four things, you become rich and successful.'

He adds two words to this train of thought: 'With ethics.'

I look at the waitress across the room, meet her eye, raise my hand slightly, the smallest of beckonings; I then look at my recording devices on the table, and at Belfort's face, his eyes, thick glossy hair short at the temples.

Four things, two things. I want to know about the two things.

'I had bankrupt values,' he says. 'Number one was money. Number two was power. Number three was sex – mostly with hookers, when my wife's back was turned. Number four was getting high on drugs. Number five was parenthood. Although I thought I was a great dad, there I am, smoking crack.'

He pauses. 'Number one, bankrupt values. Upside-down values. And the beliefs. I was allowing my beliefs that I held, core beliefs, to come from sources that were ridiculous. I'll give you an example. When I made my first $650,000 on a stock trade. I was twenty-four. What'd I do? First thing I did was buy a *white Ferrari Testarossa*. Why?'

I am nodding.

'Because Don Johnson was driving one in *Miami Vice*. Second thing I did, I took a plane out to the west coast, checked into the Regent Beverly Wilshire Presidential Suite. Why? Richard Gere did it in *Pretty Woman*.'

Richard Gere! The mention of Gere makes my heart skip. Of course, the man Belfort is referring to is actually Edward Lewis, the character Gere plays in *Pretty Woman*. Lewis is obsessed with money – until he meets a sex worker, played by Julia Roberts, who gives him a magic kiss. After the magic kiss, Lewis is no longer obsessed with money.

He *likes* it, for sure. He's just not *addicted* to it.

I look at Belfort. He says: 'The third thing, and this is really the destructive belief, was …'

For a moment he looks downcast.

'We're *so* easily brainwashed by outside forces,' he says. 'The third one, and I'd sue the bastard if I could, but I can't. You know who it was? Gordon Gekko. "Greed is good." I watched this movie, and a lot of kids my age did, and oh my God he was the coolest guy ever, he was handsome, well dressed, and I went out there, like, with this thing about the ends justifying the … greed is good, greed *cuts through*.'

Again, he pauses. 'Greed is *not* good.'

I have another urge to interject something, and I'm wondering how, exactly, to put it.

After all, what is greed? Originally, the word was used to describe the state of being really, really hungry. In ancient times, everybody had a word for it – Saxons said they were *gradag*, people from the Low Countries were *gretig*, the English said *gredig*.

Being really, really hungry is bad, right? Obviously it is.

But it's also good.

I was talking to this guy Richard Wrangham, an ape guy – he spent a lot of time living with chimps. He went into the jungle and followed the chimps around, and actually tried to eat what they were eating.

And the thing was, he said, it was horrible.

You think of chimps eating a lot of fruit, bananas and so on. Certainly that's what they'd like to eat, given the choice. But mostly they don't have the choice, because where they live, all the low-hanging fruit has already been eaten by insects and bats and monkeys with prehensile tails.

Not just the low-hanging fruit – the *high*-hanging fruit as well. So the chimps have to eat these gourds and leaves. And these gourds and leaves, they're tough to chew. The leaves are leathery, and the gourds are sort of rubbery, it's like chewing a Pirelli tyre. These chimps, they need to spend hours chewing every day. Like four or five hours, just chewing. That's why they've got such big jaws.

And Wrangham says, if you have to spend half your time climbing around, hoping against hope for a banana, but mostly looking for rubbery things, and leathery things, and then maybe another third of your time sitting on a branch chewing, you don't have much time left over.

Chewing is pretty much your job. You get up in the morning, go to work, chew all day. You can 'make a living', as Wrangham puts it – but only just.

Still, the craziness engendered by being *gredig* sharpens you. It forces you to think new thoughts. Over the years, some chimps – maybe the descendants of the ones who got good at poking sticks into the beehives – get a bit better at thinking new thoughts. Their brains develop a capacity for looking at objects and seeing them in a new way. A branch can look like a stick. A stick can look like a tool.

These chimps already know that cooked gourds and tubers, the ones that have been burned in forest fires, taste much better.

So after every forest fire, these apes comb the area for cooked food.

And then the big thing happens. According to Wrangham, it happens two million years ago.

One day, an ape pokes a stick into the fire. This ape sees the stick as a stick, and then as a fire-making tool. It's like the moment you stop seeing two faces, and start seeing a vase. Faces become vase. Stick becomes taper. You can *make more fire*. Something for nothing!

It can't be true. But it *must* be true ...

For millions of years, nothing much has happened. But now something does happen. Quickly! The apes get rich – quick. But it's not a get-rich-quick *scheme*.

The hardest you ever work is when you're not making any money.

All that foraging time, all that chewing time, they weren't getting rich. They were making a living, but only just.

And then ... they got rich quick.

Not rich exactly. But definitely rich*er*. They came down from the trees, walked upright, sat around campfires, built shacks.

And all because of greed. Greed, the driver of everything. Greed, the essence of evolution, the mother of invention. Greed, the bringer of plenty, the seeker of hidden value.

Greed, eventually the force behind technology and finance. Greed making the steam engine, the internal combustion engine, the silicon chip. Greed filling the roads and the skies. Greed extracting the oil and the rubber. Greed behind the cars and the ads for the cars, and the cameras to take the pictures for the ads, the selection of hot people in the ads, the slender limbs, the prominent cheekbones, the glossy hair, the white teeth.

Greed making it all possible – the automatic doors, the lobby, the curved bar, the bobbing boats, the recording devices on the table, the fizzy mineral water I'm about to order, the bottling factory it came from, the corporation that owns the factory, the stock issued in the corporation's name, the speculators who buy the stock, who persuade others to buy the stock, who formulate strategies for buying low and selling high, who get rich, who buy mansions and yachts, but then inexplicably feel poor, and slip into a psychological crevasse, and start to commit crime, thinking they won't get caught.

'Greed's destructive,' says Belfort. 'It's *passion* that's good. It's *ambition* that's good.'

The waitress arrives at the table. We order water and coffee. Situation normal: two men, talking volubly, dressed casually, making lofty assertions, processing midlife crises.

The waitress walks away. I look at Belfort.

I don't make my interjection.

***

Over the next couple of hours, a period that passes in a flash, an intense fugue state, Belfort tells me about the 'four things' – the 'four things that I instilled in the people that worked for me, that allowed them to soar'. The four things that will make me extremely wealthy and successful, according to Belfort – the four corners of his philosophy, of the philosopher's stone he has wrought over the years of effort and money and prison and starting again.

He talks. I listen. It feels like I'm sitting in front of a room full of people trying to persuade me. You can do it, they are saying. You can be this person, they are saying.

You can be this rich person.

The four things, it seems to me, are the things you need to master if you want to thrive, and prevail, in today's world. It's a changing world where all the low-hanging fruit has been taken, where all the stuff they tell you in school is no longer relevant, where you can't do much if you just follow orders, do what you're told, work hard, keep your nose clean; it's a world where you can't just get a normal job and then buy a nice house, and a car, and pay for your kids' tuition fees, and go on holidays, the things your parents took for granted; it's a world in which it is not good enough to be middle class, because the middle class are the new poor – the water line of poverty is creeping up.

So you need to turn yourself into a certain type of person.

'Create a compelling vision,' Belfort is saying. 'Not a goal. There's a level above goals, which is vision.'

That's the first thing.

'Learning to manage your emotions.'

That's the second thing.

'Getting to the bottom of the beliefs that are holding you back, and rooting out those beliefs.'

That's the third thing.

'Strategy.' That's the fourth thing. Basically, learning about something, how it's made of different parts, and then manipulating the parts, doing this tirelessly, until some kind of magic happens. And then you're in a different world.

Belfort trained his employees to sell things. He created a system. He perfected the system. He called it The Straight Line.

'You can't *imagine* what happened,' he says. 'It was like literally any person … someone can be as smart as a box of rocks, with no sales ability, from a poor family, told they're a loser their entire life … and six months later they'd be rich. Because it was a sure-fire system.'

He thinks back to a day long ago. The day he knew his system was going to work. He was in a crummy office in the exurbs of Long Island. 'I was like, oh my God. Oh my God. I looked around the room. There were twelve guys there. And I said, Oh my God. I just hit on something like I discovered fire.'

***

Belfort made millions, then tens of millions.

But he felt *poor*. He turned to crime.

Why?

This is something we discuss now, and will discuss later, in this hotel and in other hotels, in this city and other cities. Sometimes I will think he understands exactly what he did, and sometimes I will think he does not. Sometimes I will think I understand exactly what he did, and sometimes not.

He says: 'What I didn't take into account is that my own success caused the stock to rise, which created more success. The clients

were like, holy shit! What else you got? I'll give you two million –
what do you have for two million? So, all of a sudden, it's getting
worse for me. I don't have things to sell, so I'm forced to sell shady
products.'

This is one way of looking at it. He created a contraption with
many moving parts, not all of which he could control.

'It grew far bigger and faster than I ever thought it would,' he
says. 'So I was in this desperate run trying to find things to sell.
I couldn't keep up with the demand. I went on a treadmill trying
to desperately create product.'

He'd drilled down. He'd hit a deep seam of other people's greed.
A geyser of greed, spurting all over the place. Totally lascivious! But
nowhere for the greed to go. That's another way of looking at it.

'Unfortunately I met this guy.'

He was desperate. He couldn't let people down. Not the clients.
Not the brokers – the company he had built. His company! Stratton
Oakmont! That's another way of looking at it.

'He was nice, this guy. He showed me a way of creating stock
that was very illegitimate. And at that time I should have walked
the other way.'

So he crossed a line. 'I don't want to point the finger at anyone
but myself. You know like an ostrich who puts his head in the sand?
I was sort of doing that myself.'

He says: 'I wasn't looking to *hurt* anybody.'

And: 'Just like the financial crisis. Once they started on the road
of selling these crappy mortgages …'

And: 'The way I relate it now, the decisions you make in the
beginning dictate what happens down the road. You can't be half
pregnant when it comes to ethics and integrity. You just can't.'

And: 'I said to myself, when I stepped over that line, I said, I'll
do it, and I'll step back, and I won't do *that* any more …'

And: 'People do it on Wall Street every day. They're doing it
right now.'

Most of what he did was perfectly legal. There's a line between
legal stock manipulation and illegal stock manipulation. It's a fine
line. That's another way of looking at it.

'What becomes illegal, OK, is if I …' He's talking about the fine line. 'I should have done a wider distribution. But because I took that stock, and put it in ratholes, and kept control of it, that's the illegal part. Everything else is legal.'

Ratholes! Places where you hide stock, in order to take it off the market, in order to increase its value. You pretend other people are buying it out of their own free will. But really you're paying people to buy it, and then to sell it, precisely when you want them to. By doing this, you can create a false picture of the value of the stock. You can make it look better than it is.

Sometimes he calls this process 'flipping the new issue'. Flipping – a word people use to describe their own fraudulent actions. Flipping is an action caused by a flipper, rather than, say, a hand. A flipper flips. A hand manipulates. When you think of a flipper, you think of a jerky movement. It doesn't sound so bad.

'OK,' he says, 'I made a mistake and allowed things to get ahead of me. The big mistake I made is I should have *slowed down* the growth of my business.'

But then he thought about the brokers at Stratton Oakmont.

'The hungry mouths!'

And he thought about the clients.

'Clients are greedy too. It's like everyone along the way is in some way complicit.'

There was mayhem. He was caught up. That's another way of looking at it. He says, of his clients: 'Here's the insanity of human nature. They'd open up an account with us. We'd send them a letter saying, the stocks we sell are crap. They're speculative. You can't buy them anywhere else. If you invest a dollar in this, you'll probably lose it. It was the *ugliest* letter. Not one person even cared. Made 'em want to buy it more.'

The greed of these people! The geysers of greed!

'Human nature,' he says.

He sold stock. Made it look better than it was. Well, he'd done that before. He'd used good angles, clever lighting. Then he crossed the fine line. This was not just using good angles and clever lighting. This was actual photoshopping. That's another way of looking at it.

He bought the country pile. Then the porn mansion. He met his second wife at the porn mansion. By now he was defined by money. He was inseparable from it. He had the suits and the watches and the cars he'd seen in the glossy magazines. His watches cost as much as other people's cars. His cars cost as much as other people's houses.

One day he's hosting a party. Nadine Caridi comes to the party. Like the watches and the cars, he's seen her in the glossy magazines.

'She walks in, she was this famous model, we exchanged a look, and ... you know that look?'

He left his wife.

He had crossed the fine line. His company was growing. More brokers, more hungry mouths to feed, more money, more fraud. Money the solution, and also the problem. Psychologically, he hit the black ice. I want to talk about the black ice. I sense he wants to talk about it, too.

He says: 'Hookers were a big part of the culture at Stratton. There were these bachelor parties. One bachelor party was more disgusting than the next. It was a game of like, you know ... limbo. How low can you go?'

Of his second marriage: 'You chip away, and chip away, and the next thing you know, there's nothing left of the statue. For us, I think the problem was, from the beginning, the entire relationship was something that wasn't pure. When I look back on those years, the only purity in my life ... was my children. Everything else was somehow corrupted, bought, paid for, bribed – including my wife.'

I mention the prostitutes. He says it didn't happen immediately. It was a case of slippage. 'You run a bathtub of piping hot water. And you stick your toe in the bath. Fuck, it's so hot, right? Five minutes later, you're submerged under the water. And it feels just fine.'

Of Nadine: 'I never cheated on her, except with hookers. That was the rationalisation back then. I said, I don't really cheat on her. They're only hookers. They're mercenaries. They're not civilians. I never cheated on her with a civilian.'

How many prostitutes? 'Over the years? Hundreds upon hundreds upon hundreds upon hundreds. Maybe a thousand. A lot. A *lot*. And I never caught anything.'

He found a way to make money. He made millions. He felt poor. He crossed a line. Prostitutes, fraud, drugs. Cocaine and Quaaludes. Then things got worse. He abused his wife. 'There was the low point where I got violent. I'm not a violent guy, I don't look like a violent guy. I'm not.'

And: 'The last fight I had was in fourth grade.'

And: 'So, I'm not a guy who goes round hitting anybody.'

And: 'But, give someone cocaine for three months, and, you know, no sleep, and enough 'ludes, and ... I don't really know what I was doing.'

And: 'You know, I just, you know, we had this struggle, and I pushed her, and she fell down a couple of steps, and she hurt her ribs, and she called the police, and I was put in jail for, you know, domestic abuse, and I went to rehab and tried to commit suic—'

He cuts the last word in half. He took a fistful of morphine pills and passed out. He had his stomach pumped. 'When you're at a point in your life when you're so fucking fed up, and you're so ...'

There's a pause. 'I can't look back at that life I used to live and find anything good about it. I can't. I never romanticise about my past. I never try to say to myself, oh, it wasn't so bad.'

Sitting here in the bar of the Chelsea Harbour Hotel, a hundred million dollars in debt, he sums up his former life.

'It sucked,' he says. 'It was evil.'

***

Two days later, I'm in a conference room in the Hilton hotel in central Manchester.

I'm listening to 'I've Gotta Feeling' by the Black Eyed Peas.

I love this song.

I know the video: the stripped clean beats as a corona of light flashes between perfect slender female thighs, a back view of the legs, Hollywood at night, girls on the prowl, Mary Janes, patent shoes with a strap, shoes and legs, hips and heels, and the stripped beat is so insistent, picked out and sharp, tight, tight!

It's about going out, about the anticipation of going out, getting ready for something, getting your hair and face ready, looking at your face in the mirror, running your hands over your own flesh, imagining a moment, that precise moment when you are unleashed, when you let go, when you 'go out and smash it', when you 'spend it up', when you 'paint the town'.

The beat lags and kicks – uh! – and the song takes off, an orgasm waiting to happen, an ejaculation of dollars, a fever dream of desire, the story behind the song being that Will.I.Am, the singer in the Black Eyed Peas, hears a David Guetta track in a club, loves it, calls Guetta on the phone, and asks him if he, Will.I.Am, can send some lyrics, and will Guetta come up with some beats, and Guetta does, he comes up with these slashing clean beats, he's been working on his dance tracks for years and years, is entering middle age, a good-looking French guy, doing pretty well, but you know, not the top top guy, and then there's this call from Will.I.Am, so Guetta says yes I'll give it a try, and writes the slashing clean beats, then makes, I don't know, ten million dollars maybe, or twenty million, whatever, just like that.

Twenty million. An ejaculation of dollars. Now Guetta is one of the richest musicians in the world. House in France, house in Ibiza, house in California, house in Dubai. Travels the world in a private jet.

As the song beats and pumps, I'm looking at a billboard. It's a picture of Belfort surrounded by various signifiers of wealth – a private jet, an Aston Martin, a helicopter. Belfort himself appears in the picture, wearing a black suit, a red tie and Ray-ban sunglasses. It is almost, but not quite, parodic – very like the cover of his book, which depicts Belfort, arms crossed, emerging from a pile of banknotes, flanked by a beautiful woman, a yacht and a helicopter.

On the billboard are the words: 'Extreme Wealth and Success with Jordan Belfort'. On the book, in contrast, are the words 'The

Wolf of Wall Street', and, below this, 'How Money Destroyed a Wall Street Superman'.

In other words, the billboard and the book cover are almost identical to look at. But they're sending quite different messages.

Or are they?

The book cover appears to say: 'This may look good, but watch out – in reality, it's evil.'

The billboard says: 'This looks good – and don't worry, it is good!'

Something doesn't quite add up here, and I'm trying to work out what it is, exactly, when the music stops and the door opens and Belfort walks in – strides in, I should say; he's walking fast, with real purpose.

Black suit, white shirt, black shoes, no tie.

He starts to tell us the story of his life. He sold ice creams on the beach when he was a kid. He sold meat and fish from a truck. His meat and fish company went bust. He didn't want to be a dentist. Loved selling. Invented the Straight Line system.

He says: 'Making money is simple, if you know how.'

And: 'I could take any frog – not that you're a frog. Boom, you're a prince.'

And: 'We tell a brilliant story about why we can't get what we want. Write this down. What stops you from getting what you want is the bullshit story you tell yourself about why you can't get it.'

And: 'Yes or yes?'

He stalks the conference room – a general addressing troops. There are theatrical flourishes. 'That's what poor people do!' he says at one point. He talks about people who are 'wealth-challenged'.

He says: 'You can leave now! You're wasting your time if you're walking around in a disempowered state! It's absolutely worthless! You need a psychology for wealth and success!'

The four things. The Straight Line. Take the bull by the horns. Act! 'Write this down,' he says. 'Wealthy people live by the tenet: I am responsible for my world. Success-challenged people – the world happens to them.'

He builds to a climax. Then another. 'Wealthy people,' he says, 'make decisions quickly. What do success-challenged people do?

"Well, I don't know, maybe." You got that? Rich people go for it! They go for it! They take shots. They say: "What's the worst that can happen?"'

'Shit,' he says, 'doesn't travel at the speed of light. It travels at the speed of shit.'

I am scribbling notes. He talks about Warren Buffett – after Bill Gates, or maybe Gates and one other guy, the richest person in the world. Buffett is the rich guy's rich guy.

'Warren Buffett', I write in my notebook, and then I draw a square around the name, and then I draw another square around the first square, and draw lines between the corners of the squares, and keep on going, so it looks like the words are on the top of a flat-topped pyramid. I keep looking at Belfort, and at the billboard featuring Belfort. I'm still trying to work out what it is about the billboard. It's nagging away.

Belfort is talking about conditioning. He says, 'We were conditioned, my friends, to be average.'

Then he says, 'There's only one way to get rich in this world. Quick.'

Again, the light goes on in my head, a moment of clarity, a rush of excitement, I love this feeling, want it to last; I want the light to stay on, want to keep it on.

Afterwards, Belfort does a book signing, and tries to get people to sign up for a three-day seminar, which costs £1,500. You can also order the 10-hour Straight Line DVD course, also £1,500.

***

The next day, we travel on the train from Manchester to Birmingham. He always travels first class, so I have to upgrade my ticket. He's wearing sunglasses, jeans, a polo shirt.

In the station, Belfort asks me if I'm afraid of anything – and, if so, what I'm afraid of. For a moment, I don't want to tell him. Not because I'm ashamed, but because I don't want to think about this particular thing, at this particular moment. But then I do tell him.

Heights, I say.

Just saying it, allowing the thought to pass between us, to become public, is mildly disturbing to me. It's the fear of the ledge, the rope bridge, the sheer cliff. But really it's the fear of something else. It's the fear of the brain becoming twisted, inverted, and now you can't stop thinking of harming yourself, letting go, just stepping out into thin air.

'Heights?'

I nod.

'I can help you with that.'

I move my head around, scanning for something, anything.

'You wanna do this? You have to imagine the thing that scares you, and then imagine you're looking at yourself from a distance.'

I am nodding and looking at a point beyond his head.

'Imagine yourself on a ledge,' he says.

I focus my eyes on the departures board, the lists of cities, platforms.

I say: 'Yes.'

And: 'Yes ...'

And: 'Our train!'

The moment passes.

On the train, we sit in the slightly more comfortable seats. We settle down and talk about the global financial crisis of 2008. 'A wholesale betrayal of the public trust.' That's his verdict. Also: 'Fraud being committed on every level.'

We agree on what happened. Financial products were dressed up to look better than they actually were. It was a beauty pageant. Mortgages dressed up like Victoria's Secret Angels.

'No one knew how bad it would be,' he says. 'I did. I knew how bad it would be.'

We go past former factories and warehouses, barns, fields, former kilns, more former factories.

'The sad thing is,' he says, 'I would have done all right, I would have been worth billions right now. You know, 95 per cent of what I did was legit, and I had this 5 per cent of flipping the new issue. If I wouldn't have done that? I would have made a little bit less.

Instead of making fifty million I would have made thirty million, and then I would have made a *billion* afterwards.'

He considers this. 'That's why I say when you persuade people, if you do it unethically, you'll make money, and in the end you'll destroy yourself and blow up. That's what happened to me. It was going off course that cost me. I didn't make more money by going off course – I made less! That's the irony of the whole thing.'

He was sentenced to four years. He served twenty-two months. 'An interesting sentence,' he says. 'Long enough to make it a bad thing, but not long enough to really take me and disrupt me to the point of disrepair.'

We rattle along. 'The problem on Wall Street is this,' he says. 'You're not creating anything. You're not building anything. There's no satisfaction. When you've written a book, or a really good piece, you look at it, and it's your creation. You get satisfaction that goes far beyond the money that you get. I never felt so satisfied as when I finished my book. I don't really enjoy writing that much. It's a struggle for me. When I speak, I don't struggle. It comes out naturally. When I write, I struggle. The point is, when I wrote my book, there was a certain pride for a job well done. That doesn't exist on Wall Street. The only barometer you have for a job well done is money.'

He says: 'You get exorbitant amounts of money. And then the money has no meaning.'

And: 'So what you do, you try to attach meaning to the money by buying possessions. People buy houses. They're not big enough. They buy bigger houses. They have one Ferrari – no, I need two Ferraris. I have a boat, I need a yacht, I need a house in the Hamptons. How many maids do you have? I have twelve. You have six. How big is my kid's birthday party?'

And: 'If I said to you now, what d'you make last year? You'd say *excuse me*? Oh, you're a writer. What d'you make? What'd they pay you? What was your income last year from writing?'

And: 'You'd look at me like I was kinda rude. But on Wall Street it's the only question you ask someone. Hey, what'd you gross last year? Oh, a million four. Uh, two million four.'

And: 'If I asked you, you'd be like: what are you on?'

I ask him about going to jail. What did he tell his children?

'It was the day before New Year's ... I had to report to jail on January 2nd. And you know, the kids, said hey, I'm coming over to speak to you, it's something important, and the kids came down, hey Dad, you know, what's up, what's going on, is something wrong, I'm like yeah ... there's a problem.'

He says: 'You know what happened many years ago? I made some serious mistakes in life, and when you make mistakes, you know, there are consequences. You can't do things, you can't, uh, take money off other people, what did I say exactly? I could reconstruct it. When you make mistakes in life, you've gotta pay. I have to go away for a while. I have to go to jail.'

And: 'My daughter frickin' lost it right there. She's on my lap. My son's on my lap. He started to cry. I started to cry. My wife ...'

And: 'I'm crying right now.'

And: 'They cried, I hugged them.'

A tear seeps out from under the lens of his sunglasses.

He says: 'I'm actually crying, thinking about my kids.'

***

Evening. I'm looking at the billboard. Aston Martin, helicopter, private jet. Belfort wearing sunglasses. I'm thinking about the thing that was nagging away at me about the pictures on the book cover and the billboard.

One says that money is good. The other says it's evil. But they're the same. It worries me.

It has worried me for a while.

The music starts up. The clean beats. The sense of anticipation. Money and sex. Shoes and legs. The voice of Will.I.Am. The beats of David Guetta. Will.I.Am sings about anticipation, about desire, about being unleashed.

Belfort appears. Black suit. White shirt. Black shoes. No tie. Sharp as a pin. A whirlwind. We scribble notes.

'There's only one way to get rich,' he says. 'Quick.'

3

Back home, I write my piece on Belfort. It takes more than a day. If you could see the entire process speeded up, it would look like a man running around a house, alighting every so often at the kitchen table, as the room gets light and dark and then light again. I press Send. Then I go for a walk.

On the walk I think about the first line of my piece.

Jordan Belfort is telling me how to get rich.

I walk along, thinking about getting rich.

The thing is, it's not about working hard. It's about *avoiding* work. You can't get rich by working. This should be obvious.

But it's not.

It's a cloudy morning. I walk along a path and up a hill. It's a gentle incline. I'm getting that special feeling you get when you stride along, one foot in front of the other, in the fresh air.

You don't get rich by working – why is this not obvious?

Because most people don't see it. Most people don't believe it.

It's not what you learn in school.

I march upwards, thinking about what you learn in school. The sun is starting to filter through the clouds.

Work hard – that's one of the main lessons. Work hard, respect the current arrangements, and you will be rewarded.

But what they tell you is exactly wrong. It's the bull's eye of wrongness.

Pass exams in this and that. Write your CV. Apply for a job, along with everybody else. Hope you're chosen. And then, when you are chosen, work hard.

Wrong, wrong, wrong!

It's a recipe for putting yourself at a disadvantage. It's a recipe for learning how to be a disadvantaged person – in other words, a poor person. And this is what they teach – this is supposed to help you! But it doesn't help you. It *hinders* you.

They are teaching you how to be poor!

Once you see this, it can't be unseen.

The education system is a factory to make you think like a poor person.

Get a job! Work hard! But the harder you work, the poorer you'll be. You'll be paid a small amount of money to do something you don't want to do. On top of this, you'll never have any time to think. You'll live a miserable life. On your deathbed, you'll feel robbed and frustrated.

Avoiding this fate – in other words, getting rich – is not about hard work. It's about learning how to *shirk* hard work.

Sure, it involves thinking. Getting rich is about learning how to think clearly, so you can devise a way to get a lot of money without doing too much work. It's about finding a short cut – about getting results with maximum efficiency.

It's about seeing a way to do things that hasn't been done before. It's about inventing something new. It's about making new tools.

And what's a tool? A tool is a way of avoiding work. A tool is a device that will give you an unfair advantage.

At first, a new tool looks wrong. It looks wrong precisely *because* it gives you an unfair advantage. Think of a lever. You get more from less. You get leverage. It looks like a trick.

At first, any new tool looks like a trick. It looks unfair. It looks exploitative.

But that's the point. That's exactly what it *is*. That's what it needs to be. It needs to be unfair. It needs to be exploitative. A tool is something that gives you an unfair advantage, so you don't need to work so hard.

A tool is something that changes the odds in your favour.

If you want to get rich, you have to look for ways to invent new tools, in order to change the odds in your favour.

To do this, you need to learn how to think clearly.

I arrive at the top of the hill, striding along, feeling the special feeling.

It's all so simple!

I've seen something. Now I can't unsee it.

Walking along the ridge of the hill, looking down at the canopy of trees, I can see something else. Or rather, I can *imagine* something else.

The apes.

Two million years ago, apes began to turn into humans. But how? They spent their whole day climbing trees and chewing rubbery leaves.

They were medium-sized animals in the middle of the food chain. They could make a living, but only just.

But then something happened. An ape did some clear thinking. It saw a fire. It saw a stick. Why not put the stick in the fire? If you put the stick in the fire, you'll get more fire.

It can't be true! It *must* be true! It –

And who is that ape? It's Belfort, at the exact moment when he pictured the Straight Line. It's Alan Sugar, having tea with his mother-in-law, at the exact moment when he looked at the butter dish. It's Howard Schultz in the Italian espresso bar. It's Felix Dennis looking at all those geeky guys lining up outside the Leicester Square cinema.

It can't be true. It *must* be true …

What the ape sees is this: the fire itself wants to make more fire. The ape does not know why. But it sees what it needs to see. The fire is hungry. The fire wants to eat the stick.

And now the ape has several new tools. One is a weapon. One is a heating system. One is a cooking range.

The odds have changed in the ape's favour.

Is this fair? Of course not. It's not fair on the lions and tigers who eat the apes.

It's not fair on the monkeys and the lemurs and the birds who compete with the apes for territory and food.

It won't be fair on the creatures who build their homes in the forest. They will be cooked. They will be eaten.

Thinking clearly about fire means the apes don't need to live in the trees, because now they are protected by the fire.

Thinking clearly about fire also means they don't need to forage all day, because now they can cook things that would otherwise be inedible – in other words, they can outsource part of their digestive system to the fire.

Thousands of years go by. The apes change. Their guts and jaws get smaller. Their brains get bigger. Their feet get bigger.

I march along the ridge of the hill. One foot in front of the other. Striding along, feeling special. Thinking about apes turning into humans. I'm getting hot, so I take my jacket off and sling it around my arm.

And now – of course! – I remember the thing about the coats.

They didn't need to wear fur coats!

All the other mammals need to wear a fur coat, all the time – a coat that's thick enough to keep them warm on the coldest day. But this has a downside, which is that they can never take the coat off.

And the worst thing about wearing a fur coat you can't take off: it limits your movement. You can run, or walk, but only for a short time, because then you start to overheat.

But something miraculous happens when you have access to fire. You no longer need a permanent fur coat. As you evolve, your fur drops off. You learn to make clothes. And now you have a choice. When you feel yourself getting too hot, you can take your coat off. And this gives you a huge advantage.

Because now you can walk at a steady pace, for hours on end, without overheating. Which means you can stalk your prey just by walking, one foot in front of the other, until you tire them out.

Is this fair? Of course not. There they are, the prey animals – worn out, panting and sweating. And there you are, buoyed by endorphins, thinking clearly, holding your coat in one hand and an axe in the other.

Now you have an unfair advantage.
Now the odds are in your favour.

***

That's the essence of getting rich, right there. You need to look for unfair advantages. It seems so simple. On the other hand, I have a problem with the idea of unfair advantages. They seem so unfair. Somewhere deep down, I'm controlled by the idea of fairness.

But this makes no sense. For instance, I'm happy to wear clothes that have been made by people in poor countries, who, if I ever think of them, seem like they must be slaves, or something close to slaves; sometimes you hear of a factory going up in flames, and you catch a glimpse of the reality, thousands of serfs, almost but not quite slaves, making millions of pairs of jeans, or women's underwear, people in terrible health, with bad complexions, bad teeth, awful posture, not sleeping enough, not eating properly, taking no proper exercise, having no time, no real money, close to no agency, living hundreds of miles from their families, stitching skimpy pants and sexy frocks, their arthritic bones bent over sewing machines.

But of course, not every factory is a sweatshop – that's what I tell myself.

Some are not.

Although I once read a book about these factories, and they are mostly even worse than you think, because the health inspectors are corrupt.

But still I tell myself: some are not.

And I sometimes eat pigs that have been reared in concrete pens and stabbed with knives, fish caught in nets and left to gasp to death, vegetables grown by horribly cheated farmers. So really I exploit people and animals all over the world. I'm a prime exploiter; I have an easy life because I pay for thousands of people and animals to be imprisoned and beaten and suffocated and stabbed and occasionally burned to death in factory fires, hundreds of miles from their families.

But somewhere deep down, I'm controlled by the idea of fairness.
It doesn't make sense.

Actually, it does. I'm a hypocrite. Part of my mind must be a cesspit of guilt and denial, of cover-ups and pay-offs, lies and half-lies.

But I still have my standards – I feel bad about wanting, or making, too much money. The thought of wanting, or making, too much money sets off certain alarm bells. I can wash my hands of all the tortured pigs and Chinese slaves, because paying for pigs to be tortured and Chinese people to be enslaved is not taboo.

It's not good.

But it's not taboo.

On the other hand, wanting to get rich, trying to get rich, training your mind to think clearly so you can get better at seeing opportunities to get rich, being a rich person, owning a rich person's car and house, trying to make sure the odds are always in your favour so you can get even richer – somehow, according to the mechanism that controls my wealth, these things are taboo.

I want to be rich. I'd love to be rich. In my heart I know I need to be rich if I'm going to pay off all my debts and survive the rest of my life.

But the mechanism in my brain that controls my wealth does not approve of rich people. The mechanism looks at money and sees a veneer, a shiny veneer covering something murky and slimy. It expertly edits and frames my view of people who have money, to make them look bad. It tries to tell me they are sociopaths, always looking for a chance to take advantage of others – or else that they are losers, secretly miserable and lonely, who still think they're better than me, which I can't stand.

It makes me hate them so I don't have to hate myself.

I am bad. But they are worse. Compared to them, I am good. They are the problem. But I envy them. I want to be like them. But I don't want to be like them. I want to be rich but I don't want to be rich. The rich are money; they think like money, they behave like money, and money is killing us; the rich are killing us, and as they kill us, they also kill themselves, but they can't see it, they just can't see it. They are blind – that's what the mechanism says.

And even when I allow for this bias, I can't help being swayed by it. When I meet the rich and the super-rich, and go to their houses, the mechanism taints my view of them.

It also taints my view of myself – the arrogant prick that I secretly hope will be my future rich self.

I must learn to love my future rich self.

***

Belfort sends me his Straight Line course. It takes ten hours to listen to it. I listen to it. Then I listen to it again. And again. It becomes a voice in my head. It's about how to be persuasive. How to persuade other people to think a certain way. But it's also about how to persuade yourself to think a certain way.

You need to persuade yourself that you can be rich, that you want to be rich, that you will be rich. Then you must act.

Have a vision. Move towards it, using a process of trial and error. Conduct experiments. Think clearly. Don't let yourself be damaged by failure. You are a scientist, trying to make discoveries.

Take action. Learn. Take more action. Learn more. Action is fuel. Action will fuel you. There are hints of other motivators – Napoleon Hill (you won't strike oil, if you don't try to strike oil, and try again, and keep trying); Jim Rohn (give people what they want, and they will give you what you want); Zig Ziglar (give enough people what they want, and they will give you *everything* you want); and Jim Rohn again (if you keep knocking you'll find open doors), and Anthony Robbins (it's not enough to be good; you must be better than good; you must be excellent), and Richard Bandler (change your inner world, and the inner world of others, by using specific language patterns which will rewire your brain).

Don't stop learning.
Don't stop improving.
Don't stop believing.
Don't stop acting.

Belfort's voice. It pushes my buttons. It prods me. Wake up, it says.

I lie on my bed, listening to Belfort's voice. I think of the mountain of money I could have. The mountain of money I will have, must have. And, really, I must have that money. Without that money, I am screwed. So I must have it. I will have it. I will persuade the world to give it to me. The world owes it to me. Give me my money!

Give me my money!

I lie on my bed and listen to Belfort's voice and think about my money. The money I must and will have. I need to look inside my own head and locate all the things that are stopping me from getting my money.

What is stopping me? Negative thoughts. The negative memes emanating from the mechanism that lies deep inside my brain. These memes are parasites, parasites that want to hold me back, pin me down; they are like an army of tiny little people, swarming, their tiny little hands clawing at my face, their tiny little feet standing on my shoulders, their tiny little mouths whispering in my ears.

Don't do it, they are saying.

Don't climb the mountain.

I am on my back, listening to Belfort's voice. I picture him walking into the room. Black suit, white shirt, black shoes, no tie.

Do it, he says.

And: 'The only thing that stops you from getting what you want in life is the bullshit story you tell yourself about why you can't have it.'

I'm lying flat. Looking upwards through my window at a patch of blue sky. Trying not to tell myself the bullshit story.

***

I must go to see Matt Ridley.

Imagine you could take a pill that stopped you feeling bad about money and wealth.

Let's say you want to get rich. But something's holding you back.

So you go to a money doctor. He looks at the mechanism in your brain, and diagnoses *Allergia divitiae,* a condition in which you feel uneasy or guilty about making money.

The illness makes you feel that wanting to be rich is morally wrong, or destructive, or even evil. It makes you see rich people in a negative light. This condition is systemic – most of the time, you're not even aware of it. Some doctors class it as a form of mild depression. Others see a spectrum; on parts of this spectrum, many sufferers can live what appear to be relatively normal lives. But they will always be poor.

Luckily, there's a pill you can take.

When you swallow this pill, the world looks like a different place. You feel differently about money. It's no longer dirty or evil. On the contrary – it's great. You begin to think that money has contributed more to the cause of human happiness than anything else – *anything* else in the world.

More than Greenpeace. More than Friends of the Earth. More than a thousand Florence Nightingales or Mother Theresas.

Money is the best thing ever!

It's right up there with God.

Of course, this pill does not exist. But if it existed in human form, it would be Matt Ridley.

Ridley is pretty rich. He's an aristocrat; he went to Eton and Oxford; his father went to Eton and Oxford; his grandfather went to Eton and Oxford; his great-grandfather went to Eton and Oxford; his great-great-grandfather went to Harrow and Oxford; he owns or part-owns a fossil-fuel company and has many other business interests; he was the Chairman of Northern Rock, a bank that crashed in the financial crisis and was then bailed out; he writes a column for the *Wall Street Journal*, he's a doctor of zoology, he lives in a big mansion with an exquisite lake he refers to as a 'sky mirror'. So, yes, pretty rich.

But there's something about him.

He believes that, if you think clearly, you will see that the world is becoming a better place. If you are rational, you will become an optimist. That's the subject of his scintillating book *The Rational Optimist*.

I say scintillating for a particular reason: it creates sparks in the mind. It's one of those books that makes the reader feel clever.

The Rational Optimist asks a big question. It asks the single most puzzling question about the human race.

Why did we suddenly colonise the planet? What happened?

Apes learned to control fire. They came down from the trees. They turned into people. These people made axes and spears. They lived in shacks.

And that was it, for about a million years.

That's puzzling, right? For a million years, there was no progress. Just the same axes, the same spears, the same shacks.

These people were a lot better off than apes. They didn't need to chew the whole time. They cooked. They hunted. They talked to each other.

But they stayed the same for forty thousand generations. Culturally, they were stuck – like, say, bears.

Bears stand at the top of waterfalls, catching salmon. They've always done that. In all that time, they haven't used rods, or lures, or nets. They don't smoke the salmon. They don't poach it, or freeze it, or store it in cans.

And they never will. They'll always just stand at the top of the waterfall and try to catch the salmon with their paws.

The bears are stuck.

And for a million years, we were stuck, too.

But then everything changed. Quickly.

About 70,000 years ago, we stopped being stuck. What happened?

As Ridley points out, it had nothing to do with our brains getting bigger. They were already big. And it wasn't about language, because we already had that.

It was something we did.

We started to swap things with each other.

That's what Ridley says. And swapping things, it turns out, is magic. It causes a sort of nuclear reaction, and there's a particular reason for this, a perfectly logical reason.

When you swap things with other people, you no longer need to do everything for yourself.

Which means you can spend more time doing the stuff you're good at.

And when you do the stuff you're good at, you get really good at it. You think more clearly. You become inventive. You invent new tools.

The more you exchange, the more new tools you invent.

Now think about why this actually works.

Let's say I have a talent. I can catch ten fish an hour, and you can only catch three. For me, fishing is not hard work, because I'm good at it. For you, it's a slog.

At some point, I'll want to pay you, in fish, to do something for me, so I can spend more time fishing.

That's the cornerstone of economics. The wealthy person, seeing an opportunity to get even wealthier, will want to make a deal.

The interesting thing is that, when we make this deal, we're both better off. Why? Because, in order to get you to stop fishing and do something for me – like building a shack – I need to offer you more fish, per hour, than you can catch yourself.

I'm happy because now I can spend more time doing what I'm good at, which is fishing; I don't need to build my own shack. And you're happy because now you get to bring home more than three fish per hour.

I fish; you build shacks. Immediately, we're both better off. And the benefits don't stop there. If I spend more time fishing, I start to invent better ways to fish. And you start to invent better ways to build shacks.

Talented people always have a surplus. And that surplus becomes a form of credit – from the Latin *credo*, which means I believe, or trust.

And that belief, or trust, begins to function as money.

And then someone invents actual money, and the process speeds up.

With actual money, everybody can exchange with everybody else. That's because everybody is willing to swap things for money, which is, in turn, because money can be turned into anything.

Swapping things makes people richer, and leads to innovation, which makes people richer still. So if money encourages exchange, then money is a good thing.

That's the Ridley pill. Exchange is the mother of invention. Money is the midwife.

The more we exchange, the more we specialise; the more we specialise, the more we innovate; the more we innovate, the more we exchange.

Ridley calls this process *auto-catalytic*. It's self-reinforcing, like an addiction.

Meanwhile the world gets better, faster and faster. The spear becomes the gun; the pelt becomes the coat; the shack becomes the mansion; the cowrie shell becomes the chunk of gold, the coin, the banknote, the line of credit.

From the Latin *credo* – I believe.

Swapping is good. Money helps you swap. Therefore money is good.

I believe.

The pill soothes my troubled mind like a drug.

And yet. Something worries me. It's like a grain of sand in my eye.

The grain of sand is the bank.

The bank that crashed.

Of course, Ridley didn't crash it.

Banks are not cars. He wasn't the driver.

It crashed.

He was the chairman.

That's the grain of sand.

***

My Belfort article is published. I sit at the kitchen table and look at the magazine. I pick up the magazine and put it down and pick it up again.

I flick the pages of the magazine with my thumb, so I can see flashes of what's inside. Blue sea, red lips, pink flesh, white teeth – and what looks like money, piles of money, thousands of banknotes floating in a cloud, dropping from the sky, an image we must all carry in our heads, in some ways our deepest desire, but also a sort of fear, the fear of money getting everywhere, money in the wrong places, money in wheelbarrows, the social fabric torn, fascists on the way.

I turn the pages.

A few pages in, there's an interview with Kate Winslet. Kate says: 'I don't bring glossy magazines into the home' – on this issue, she agrees with Ted Bundy. She's in a white shirt, open to midriff level, and a black bra, like the photographer is some kind of snooper.

I turn the pages very slowly.

One more, one more.

My heart skips. Here it is.

I'm looking at a double-page spread, a picture of Belfort – dark suit, white shirt, dark hair. He's sitting in a very expensive-looking silver sports car. A cloud of money is floating above the car.

And ... Jesus! He really reminds me of someone. It's Edward Lewis – the Richard Gere character in *Pretty Woman*!

Like Lewis, Belfort is in a silver sports car. Like Lewis, he's wearing a dark suit with a white shirt. Like Lewis, he's in Beverly Hills, about one minute's driving time from the Regent Beverly Wilshire, where Lewis stayed in the film, where Belfort says he went to stay, because he identified with Lewis.

This picture has been taken on one of those palm-tree streets – possibly Hillcrest Drive, or Bedford Drive, or North Linden Drive. Does North Linden have palms? I must check with Google Earth.

Anyone who's seen *Pretty Woman* will remember the early sequence in which Gere, as Lewis, gets into the silver sports car and drives, first up and down, and then round and round, looking for the Regent Beverly Wilshire. He gets lost. He finds himself on the wrong side of town. He stops to ask directions. A sex worker, Vivian Ward, played by Julia Roberts, walks up to Edward's car. She says she'll show him the way – for a fee.

In the photograph, Belfort has a strange expression on his face. He looks lost.

But to me, the weirdest thing about this picture is that I *know* this street, I've walked down this street – in fact, I've walked down this street while thinking about Edward Lewis.

Go back a few years, and remove Belfort from the picture. Then insert me into the picture. I've checked the street on Google Earth. It's Bedford Drive.

Go back in time. I'm walking along Bedford Drive thinking about Edward Lewis. Also Julian Kay, Zack Mayo, Jack Moore – all versions of the preening, slightly contemptuous, ultimately self-loathing guy Richard Gere mostly plays. In twenty-four hours' time, I will interview Gere.

The interview will not go well.

Picture me walking along the broad, pale sidewalk, under the tall palms, the beautiful palms, with a precise smell in my nostrils, a perfume of warm weedkiller and ozone and traffic fumes, top-notch smog, it always gets me, this smell; it's the exact smell of walking slowly past very expensive houses in all styles, a cartoon of suburbia, with bright green turf, lawn-sprinklers, Mexican gardeners clipping and tending, Italian and German cars at rest or cruising past, a vision of luxury, peaceful and also sinister, you keep thinking anything can happen at any time, but only because this is a very over-filmed part of the world, and we all know what stories say about rich suburbia, they say this peace and luxury does not come for free, you pay for it, and the price is slashers and criminals, or even something alien, something we have not yet imagined, a novel type of zombie or robot, or a beautiful woman, designed by extraterrestrials to be insanely attractive, roaming the streets, looking for unprotected sex.

Or, of course, mobsters – like the crime kingpin Bugsy Siegel, as played by Warren Beatty in the movie *Bugsy*, who cruises these very streets, and when he finds a house he likes, he knocks on the door and tells the owner he wants to buy it on the spot – or, rather, not that he *wants* to buy the house, but that he's *going* to buy the house, and that's that. And he does. (Although I'm not sure that happened in real life – in real life, Siegel lived in a house on Mulholland Drive, a classic porn mansion called Castillo del Lago, while he raised the money to fund his big project, the Flamingo Hotel and Casino in Las Vegas. Still, his girlfriend lived in Beverly Hills, on North Linden Drive, which is where, after a frantic few weeks of

borrowing money, and borrowing more money, and being unable
to pay the interest on the money he'd borrowed, he was shot twice
in the head and also in the arm and chest; one of the bullets entered
his head at an odd angle and shot his eyeball across the room. It was
1947. The killer was hiding in the front garden. *Bugsy*, the movie,
teaches us the classic gangster lesson. The gangster wants too much;
he can't help himself; he will die; watch out, because he is you.)

Bugsy had a very powerful gut feeling that gambling had a big
future, a much bigger future than people thought – he could see
gambling moving into the mainstream, a normal leisure activity.
It's in our blood, is what he could see. But he went broke before his
own gamble paid off; his last sensation must have been a whizzing
or buzzing in the area behind the eyes, a momentary migraine that
seems to pass the very moment it arrives.

Anyway, I'm walking along, under the palms, smelling the
expensive smog. Physically and mentally, I'm not in great shape.
Like Bugsy, I'm deep in debt, and this is making me anxious. I've
been treating the anxiety with drink and drugs. Drink, I now see,
is just another type of loan – a way of borrowing happiness from
your future self, which at some point you must pay back, plus
interest. With drugs, you can borrow larger amounts of happiness,
but the interest rates are mostly much higher. Drink is a bank loan;
drugs are a payday loan or a junk bond. With drugs, every so often
someone offers you what looks like a good deal – MDMA, for
instance. But if you read the small print, it's never quite as good as
it looks.

A bit of debt feels OK. It feels like you've entered a relationship
with someone, or maybe several people. You've got their attention,
you're on their radar, and you need to watch yourself, which is fine.
A bit more debt – still fine. A little bit more – yes, this is fine too.
At some point, you enter a strange, unreal world; something is
supporting you, but you know this thing might break under your
weight. You're in mid-air, hanging from a rope above a yawning
chasm, and you're getting heavier all the time. People are holding
on to the rope; you know your safety is important to them. But
your safety is only important to them as long as it does not threaten

88

their safety – as long as there is no possibility that you will pull them into the chasm.

For a while, you think the people holding the rope will always hold the rope.

And then you start to think they might not.

You start to think about the chasm.

Even now, I'm still trying to understand this – why I got into debt when I had a lot of money. One reason I've come up with: it's hard to see the borderline between having much more money than you need, and having an infinite amount. Part of your mind works on the principle that you have an infinite amount. You know this can't be true. But it *feels* true.

I got a lot of money for doing almost nothing. That was my job. So I did almost nothing, and spent the money. When the money was gone, I borrowed more money. Then I spent the money I borrowed. I had an expensive flat, expensive clothes; I had a girlfriend who was used to having a boyfriend who could buy expensive things. But I had no money. That was fine: I borrowed more. Then I had to pay taxes. I couldn't do that. So I let my taxes slide. And when you get a lot of money, or rather when you *have had* a lot of money, even if your current situation is that you have nothing, even if you are actually poor, you still need to pay a lot of tax, as if you still had a lot of money, when you don't. So there was that.

That's when I made an error.

The error happened when someone offered me a job. The terms of the job interested me. Instead of getting a lot of money for doing almost nothing, I'd be getting significantly less money for doing much more than almost nothing. And I liked the idea of doing much more than almost nothing. Doing much more than almost nothing, I hoped, would force me to rethink my policy of borrowing happiness by using drink and drugs. Maybe doing much more than almost nothing would be, in itself, a sort of happiness.

It would be like turning a page.

Now the debt would be a much bigger problem. The rope would be at breaking point. A mortgage, bank loans, bank charges, overdraft fees, default fees, taxes, credit cards, bills, fines on unpaid bills, penalties on unpaid fines, court cases, legal fees, envelopes containing poisonous documents. Men and women knocking on the door, asking questions about 'the missing money'.

But then, there was always the future. I would get rich in the future!

'So you'll do it?'

'It sounds great.'

'That's a yes?'

The rope was holding me. Then it wasn't.

'Yes,' I'd said.

And now I was walking beneath the tall palms, doing much more than almost nothing, walking and thinking of the chasm I was falling into, and of Zack Mayo, and Julian Kay, and Edward Lewis, the vain, contemptuous figures that Richard Gere wanted to play, for his middling money – his couple of million per movie. I was thinking of the chasm, and of Mayo and Kay and Lewis, these preening pricks, and of Gere himself, the man who played the preening pricks.

The interview would not go well.

***

Fast forward. Remove me from the picture. Put Belfort back in. He's in the street in Beverly Hills. He's sitting at the wheel of the silver sports car. There's a cloud of banknotes in, on and above the car.

I'm sitting at my kitchen table, looking at the picture. A picture of a guy in a dark suit, in a silver sports car, in Beverly Hills.

Edward Lewis, I'm thinking.

In the movie, made by the Walt Disney Company, Lewis is a corporate raider – he buys companies that don't want to be bought. He's a hostile takeover artist. When he buys the companies, he breaks them up and sells off the parts – the buildings and the land. The workers lose their jobs.

In other words, Lewis makes money by destroying American industry.

He doesn't actually do anything. He's mastered a trick, a sequence of financial moves known as a leveraged buyout. He borrows vast amounts of money, using junk bonds, basically payday loans for rich people. Then he buys shares in a company until he controls it, then he breaks the company into parts, sells the parts, pays back what he's borrowed and walks away, now much richer, leaving the world a worse place.

So Edward Lewis is the bad capitalist; he embodies the fear in the back of our minds, the fear that our system of exchange and specialisation, of supply and demand, of price discovery, of financial tools, of stocks and bonds, is finally broken.

A line has been crossed.

Lewis has got things the wrong way round. He doesn't create commodities, in order to exchange them for money, so he can buy other commodities – what's sometimes called C-M-C. He's strictly M-C-M. He goes from money to money, using the real world of people and commodities as a stepping stone. Essentially, he swaps one type of money for another type. He seems to have found a way to defy the laws of nature. He makes money by causing damage.

He's not happy. The first time we see him, he's at a party in a flashy house in the Hollywood Hills – a porn mansion, a villain's pad. Lewis is the party's guest of honour. He's not relaxed. He's on the phone, and his girlfriend is dumping him – right there and then. A human connection is being severed. Why? Because this guy is more interested in money than his girlfriend. He puts the phone down and neurotically asks someone about a stock price.

He wants money, we will come to see, for its own sake, because something is missing inside him. After a while, we see what it is. It's love. Lewis doesn't love anybody. He's even lost the ability to care about himself. The only thing he cares about is money – the very thing that is destroying his life.

He's an addict.

He leaves the mansion and gets into the silver sports car. He can't stand to be at the party, where he must talk to people and be normal. What he really wants to do is to go back to his suite at the Regent Beverly Wilshire and think about money – he's like a drug addict who can't wait to get away from everyone so he can be alone with his drugs.

So he gets in the car and drives off.

But he gets lost. He drives up into the hills, higher and higher, as dusk falls. Later, we will find out about his problems – what's made him so empty and selfish. His father dumped his mother for a younger woman. Then his mother died. So he hated his father. As soon as he could, he made a hostile corporate raid on his father's company. Then he broke the company up. Then his father died. So now he's an orphan who lives to break up companies and make money. We never find out how much he's worth. But we know he can raise a billion dollars to enact a raid.

Personally, he's probably worth about a hundred million. And all he wants is more money.

Who can help this lost soul, this modern-day Faustus? He stops to ask directions. The person he asks is Vivian Ward, a prostitute, a *sex professional* – a woman who has also, in her own way, made a Faustian pact. Edward Lewis has sold his soul. Vivian Ward sells her body, but she's fought hard to keep her soul intact. She's fallen on hard times. But she hasn't quite gone under. Edward hires her for a week. She sells him her body. But she won't kiss him on the mouth. She doesn't do intimacy.

Then, halfway through the film, she does. Vivian gives Edward the magic kiss. She gives him love, at which point he stops loving money for its own sake. Of course, they both still *like* money; *Pretty Woman* is famous for its shopping scenes. But that's OK. What's not OK is loving money *for its own sake*.

According to *Pretty Woman*, shopping is fine. Spending amounts of money that are 'obscene', and 'indecent' and 'offensive', to use Lewis's own words – that's fine too. Walking along Rodeo Drive laden with shopping bags full of designer clothes – that's also fine. Having a chauffeur-driven limo is fine. Flying in your own private jet is fine.

But one thing is not fine. The love of money *per se*. That's because the love of money ruins the world. It makes you clinically depressed. If you love money for its own sake, this depression will emanate outwards, harming and repelling everybody you know.

Pretty Woman tells us that the love of money itself, the love of money for its own sake, is a pact with the devil. It will send you to hell. You will fall further and further into the chasm. And Edward, as he mentions more than once, is terrified of heights. He's got this OCD thing; he even feels scared to go out on his balcony at the Regent Beverly Wilshire.

Metaphorically, though, he's already falling. And only one thing can break his fall – someone who has already fallen. A woman who has almost, but not quite, lost her soul.

And what I'm thinking here, as I look at Belfort sitting in the silver sports car, is that *Pretty Woman* is the most successful romantic comedy *ever made*. Millions of people loved its message.

They loved the message that money is fine, as long as you don't love it for its own sake; that Edward Lewis is a rapacious, self-hating prick, until he's saved by a fallen woman; that capitalism has reached a tipping point; that the system is broken; that the cycle of exchange and specialisation, having held up for aeons, has entered a new, destructive phase; that buying things is fine, but buying bonds in order to buy stocks in order to destroy companies in order to sell off their land in order to make yet more money is not fine.

A line has been crossed.

I like *Pretty Woman*. I identify with the second version of Edward Lewis – the man who checks out of the Regent Beverly Wilshire, having narrowly avoided the depths of hell.

The twenty-seven-year-old Belfort, on the other hand, identified with the other Edward Lewis – the man who checked *into* the Regent Beverly Wilshire.

In other words, I fell for the Disney message. Or rather, the mechanism in my brain fell for the Disney message.

The message that says: work hard, make things, pay your dues. There's no such thing as a free lunch. Don't be greedy. Don't look for short cuts. Don't seek unfair advantages. Don't exploit people. Don't rig the game in your favour. Don't be a predator. Don't be the fox in the henhouse. Don't seek opportunities for easy profit. Because if you do, you'll fall into the depths of hell.

That's what Disney says. That's also what the mechanism says.

Sitting at the kitchen table, I look at the picture of Belfort.

The silver sports car.

The cloud of money.

Maybe the money is attracted to him. Maybe it wants to stalk and kill him. Maybe both.

I look at the expression on his face. He looks anxious. He's looking over his shoulder.

I turn the page.

I read the first line of my article.

Jordan Belfort is telling me how to get rich.

My eye abseils down the page.

There's only one way to get rich, and that's quick.

My eye slides down, faster and faster.

Greed.

Gambling.

Mansions.

Sports cars.

His life fell apart.

Bang!

That's when I see how the mechanism works.

***

I'm thinking about Matt Ridley. I'm thinking about what it's like to *be* Matt Ridley.

I'm thinking about Joe Simpson. I'm thinking about what it's like to *be* Joe Simpson.

Joe wanted to climb to the top of a mountain, and he got to the top, and then something went horribly wrong for Joe.

Matt wanted his bank to make more and more money. The bank took risks, and then more risks, and then something went horribly wrong for Matt.

Joe wanted something. His feet slipped. He crashed.

Matt wanted something. The bank slipped. The bank crashed.

They were driven upwards, towards the high slopes, and now they couldn't afford to make a mistake, but they did.

They wanted something, and got what they wanted, but somewhere between wanting and getting, something inside their minds slipped, something about their thinking accelerated away from them.

There comes a point when you have no choice but to keep climbing.

Matt and Joe reached that point.

So they kept climbing.

Towards what?

Towards a psychological vanishing point.

Towards a moment of horror.

Towards their own personal tragedy, the mechanism tells me.

***

The first time I ever heard of Joe Simpson was the day I met this guy Rick. This was the summer of 1990. Margaret Thatcher was prime minister of the UK. George H.W. Bush was the new US president. *Pretty Woman* was in cinemas around the world, on its way to making $458 million, a record for a romantic comedy.

For years, my friend Callum had told me about Rick. You have to meet Rick, he said. Rick had trained as a doctor but quit at the last moment. Then he studied English literature. Rick was handsome. He had blondish hair. Girls loved Rick.

Over the years I'd picked up new pieces of information: Rick had a girlfriend, Rick split up with his girlfriend. He got a job in advertising, a nice place, a new girl. Then the news got darker. Not all was well with Rick. He'd started to have episodes of depression.

The depression came and went. When it came it was deep. But then it would go away for a while.

One day Callum said, let's go and meet Rick. So we went to Rick's place.

Rick was great. I liked Rick. He had a nice place that was slightly messy. He had a dry sense of humour. We could be friends, me and Rick. That was my exact thinking.

The three of us went out for a meal in a Greek restaurant. Then we went back to Rick's. Rick went into his bedroom and came out with a book. It was *Touching the Void* by Joe Simpson.

'You have to read this,' he said.

Callum read half of the book that night. He read the other half the next day. Then he gave it to me.

'God,' he said. 'Rick was right.'

Something was odd about the back cover of the book. Words had been blacked out with a marker pen. Rick hadn't liked the blurb on the back of the book, the way it framed the story. So he blacked bits of it out – about a quarter of the text. He thought it was better for the reader not to know in advance that something or other was going to happen.

'Rick's obsessive,' Callum said.

But then Callum agreed with Rick about the blurb.

I started reading the book that evening. It was about these two guys who went to Peru to climb a mountain. Simon Yates and Joe Simpson. They wanted to climb the west face of Siula Grande. Nobody had climbed the west face before. It was a series of ice cliffs 4,000 feet high. Some parts were vertical, some not quite vertical.

Alone in my bedroom, I tried to imagine a 4,000-foot ice cliff. Then I tried to imagine climbing that cliff. It would be like climbing the Empire State Building four times over, if the Empire State Building was made of ice.

So you'd climb as high as the top of the world's most famous skyscraper. And you'd be hanging there, joined to the ice by the points of your ice axes, one in each hand, and your crampons, the spikes on the front of your shoes.

You'd be a quarter of the way up, with three more Empire State Buildings above you.

Below you: certain death. But above you: an even more sickening sight.

Simpson and Yates climbed to 2,000 feet and rested on a rock ledge. Reading this, I felt a cold painful pulse moving from my groin to my stomach, and then upwards to my brain stem, a cold pulse of despair. I could not bear it – the thought of sitting on a rock ledge exactly halfway up. The same amount of sheer vertical emptiness above you as below. The same below as above.

I clenched my teeth. I imagined the chasm below, the chasm above.

I put the book down.

I've heard various explanations for my fear of heights. Heights fill me with uncontrollable emotions. They force my mind away from reason and towards panic. They make me feel abandoned and exposed.

Exposed to what?

Some people say a fear of heights is a survival instinct.

Others say the brain gets caught in a feedback loop.

Look down there.

Jesus, that's dangerous.

But it's not dangerous, because I'm on a balcony.

But my brain is telling me it's dangerous.

But it can't be, because it's a strong balcony. And there's a railing.

So the danger must be coming from elsewhere. The brain must know something.

Such as what?

Such as the fact that I'm planning to throw myself off.

But I'm not planning to throw myself off!

So why is my brain telling me I am?

I'm not!

But I must be!

I'm not!

Maybe I am!

Then again, this doesn't make sense, because I'm absolutely fine when I cross a road. I never imagine I'll step into the traffic, even though the traffic is super-dangerous – even though everything beyond the kerb might as well be a 4,000-foot chasm.

But in this situation I'm calm. I just wait for the lights to change. Then I look both ways, just to make sure. Then I cross.

One theory is that if you believe you're frightened of one thing, you're actually frightened of something else, something even harder to think about than the thing you think you're frightened of. So your brain becomes expert in the creation of plausible fears. I have lots of them – I'm an anxious person – and my fear of heights happens to be the most effective.

What am I really afraid of?

Halfway up the ice face, Joe and Simon made a little camp. This sparked a terrible memory for Joe. He'd camped on a ledge before, with a 2,000-foot drop below him. As he was falling asleep, the ledge broke off the mountain. Joe found himself hanging off the side of the rock face, in his socks. Just hanging there. He was held by a rope, which was tied to a peg, which he'd hammered into the rock.

He looked up.

The peg was moving.

He hung there for twelve hours, terrified, much more likely to die than to survive, until, by chance, a helicopter rescued him.

I kept putting the book down. I couldn't bear to look at it. But I pressed on, in fits and starts, towards the summit.

A few hundred feet from the summit, there's a very scary moment. Joe clambers onto a band of wet rock, 'tilted like a steep roof', and covered with a layer of snow. He can't find a foothold. But he can't stay still. He must walk up the slippery roof on the points of his crampons, with nothing to hold on to, towards an easier surface he can see up ahead. He is joined to Simon by a rope. But Simon can't see him; Simon is below the jutting band of rock.

Joe is on the slippery steep roof. To get to safety, he needs to take a few quick steps. All he has is momentum. His crampons are 'on the verge of slipping'. And suddenly he's petrified. He can't move.

But he must move. But he can't.

If he slips, he'll fall 4,000 feet. Simon will be ripped from the mountain.

Reading *Touching the Void*, I kept thinking: he's warning us. Telling us about the treacherous nature of human ambition. The black ice in the mind. Simpson and Yates wanted to achieve something nobody else had achieved. They gambled. Theirs was the classic gambler's story.

In his book *Red-Blooded Risk*, Aaron Brown, a financial risk analyst by profession, tells us that risk is the basis for storytelling.

We all instinctively understand the 'red-blooded hero', his 'hot-blooded sidekick', the 'thin-blooded person in charge' and the 'cold-blooded villain'.

Brown says: 'We admire the first two people in different ways, feel sorry for the third, and hate the fourth.'

In Brown's schema, a coward – a thin-blooded person – 'treats risks as dangers'. A thrill-seeker – a hot-blooded person – 'treats risks as opportunities'. A cold-blooded person 'treats both opportunities and dangers as risks'.

But a red-blooded person has the balance right. A red-blooded person doesn't let fear stop him from seeing opportunity. But he doesn't let ambition stop him from seeing danger.

At the beginning of *Touching the Void*, I saw Joe and Simon as red-blooded guys. They felt they could get to the top of Siula Grande. They knew it was possible.

If nothing went wrong, it was more than possible. It was likely.

But things did go wrong.

The weather was bad. They kept on climbing. Their supplies ran low. They kept on climbing. Their hands started to freeze. They kept on climbing.

Towards what?

When they got to the summit, Joe had mixed feelings. He'd got what he wanted. But he could already see he wouldn't be satisfied. Soon, he'd want something else – something bigger, better, more risky.

By this time, I was already forming a new opinion of Simpson.

He was hot-blooded.

And then something bad happened – the thing that often happens to hot-blooded guys. The thing that Rick had redacted from the blurb with his marker pen.

Joe slipped.

He saw risks as opportunities. Which made him slip.

Joe landed badly. He broke his leg. He didn't just break it. The lower part of his leg was forced up through his knee joint. His right leg no longer had a knee; the knee was a bag of smashed bones.

That's when Joe knew.

If Simon didn't help him to get down, he would definitely die. And if Simon did help him to get down, they would probably both die.

And now there was a snowstorm. A white-out.

In the white-out, Simon lowered Joe down the ice face. When Joe reached the end of the rope, he fixed himself to the ice with his ice axes and the crampon at the end of his good leg. Then Simon climbed down and repeated the procedure. He did this seven times. But then something went wrong. Simon lowered Joe over a ledge. Joe couldn't fix himself to the ice.

Joe's weight began to pull Simon off the mountain.

Simon made a calculation. If he cut the rope, Joe would fall. If he didn't cut the rope, they'd both fall.

Simon was 150 feet higher than Joe. He had 150 feet further to fall. He would die. He had a knife in his pocket. He would somehow need to pull his glove off his free hand. He'd use his teeth. Then he could get the knife.

On the end of the rope, Joe looked up. The sky was dark and he could see lights twinkling. The lights looked like gemstones, he thought.

He looked down. Below him was a crevasse. A dark hole. He didn't know how deep it was.

***

Matt Ridley's bank, Northern Rock, wasn't a famous bank. It wasn't HSBC. It wasn't Deutsche Bank. But it was ambitious. Ridley's Rock wanted to be a big lender.

Ridley's Rock did what all banks do. It borrowed money at a small rate of interest, and lent money at a bigger rate of interest. That's called the spread. And when you've got a spread, you can do two things. You can lend a smaller amount of money, and try to get a big spread. Or you can shrink the spread, and try to lend a larger amount of money.

Either way you're selling money, because that's what lending at interest is.

You sell money now, in return for more money later.

Ridley's Rock decided to shrink the spread – in other words, they decided to sell money cheaply. It's a very good way of making money. The problem is that if you sell money cheaply, you need to sell a lot of it. You need to sell money you don't have.

Selling money you don't have! Of course, all banks do this – they lend money they don't have, and charge interest, which becomes money they do have. Alchemy, you might say. A form of virgin birth, you might say. It's what all banks do. It's gambling. It's the bedrock of our society.

But Ridley's Rock went harder. Compared with the money they did have, they sold a huge amount of money they didn't have.

Selling all this money you don't have leaves you exposed. It leaves you open to the elements. But there is one thing you can do to protect yourself. You can sell more money.

Ridley's Rock was a red-blooded bank. And then, at a certain point, it became a hot-blooded bank.

Ridley's Rock was climbing the charts. It was the fifth biggest mortgage lender in the UK. Then the fourth biggest. It would eventually be the third.

Meanwhile, Jordan Belfort was in California, awaiting trial. Out on bail, he didn't know what to do. He was banned from the stock market. He didn't want to go back to selling meat and fish from a truck. But then he spotted an opportunity. Was there anything to stop him becoming a mortgage broker? There was not. Was there money to be made in the mortgage industry? Absolutely. It was the early 2000s. Interest rates were low. Banks needed to shrink the spread and lend more money.

Belfort saw an opening.

Back in the UK, Ridley's Rock was shrinking the spread and selling money like crazy, and lending an enormously large amount of money.

Every bank needs to have a certain amount of money in its coffers in proportion to the amount it lends. Think of this as fuel in the tank. The best way to get enough fuel is to build up a large pool of long-term deposits. But Matt's Rock didn't have time to build up a large pool of long-term deposits. Instead, they borrowed money, on a day-to-day basis, from hedge funds and finance companies and investment banks. As long as they could borrow short-term money, they would never run out of fuel.

It was a just-in-time machine – beautifully efficient as long as it was perpetually in motion. All they had was momentum.

Matt's Rock was a money factory, in a universe of other money factories, at the leading edge of specialisation, designed to exchange desire and trust for different shades of desire and trust; money arriving on one conveyor belt and being diverted to another conveyor belt; money gushing; money being bottled; money coming into harbour and money setting sail; money getting ready, getting its hair and face ready, money looking at itself in the mirror, trying on different costumes; money hitting the streets, money smiling at the bouncer, money walking beyond the velvet rope; money sauntering up to the bar, money the pick-up artist, money staying up late, money spawning, replicating with itself, money not sleeping, five minutes in the shower and ready for work in the morning.

But what would happen if the just-in-time machine ran out of fuel?

Back in California, the opportunity Belfort had spotted was called 'refi' – refinancing mortgages. Interest rates were low, which meant that lots of relatively prosperous people were paying more for their houses than they needed to. All you had to do was knock on doors and persuade these people to switch to a cheaper lender. Totally legitimate. Belfort made a ton of money by helping people.

Helping people by squeezing the banks.

And what do squeezed bankers do? They get creative. In America, the squeezed bankers sold bad mortgages, with high interest rates, to poorer and poorer people. Then they mixed the bad mortgages with good mortgages, and sold these mixed bundles, called CDOs, to hedge funds and pension funds and mutual funds and finance companies and investment banks. But everything was fine, because all this lending to poor people was creating demand for houses, and the increased demand was making house prices go up, and as long as house prices were going up, the poor people could pay their mortgages, because they could always borrow money.

It looks like a good system – putting poor people on a conveyor belt, lending them money, turning their mortgages into CDOs, and then selling the CDOs to hedge funds and investment banks. For a while, everybody's happy. The poor people get houses. The lenders get money for selling the CDOs. The hedge funds and investment banks get a steady stream of the poor people's high interest payments from the CDOs, which the poor people can pay because their house prices keep going up.

Everybody's happy as long as those house prices keep going up.

The system is a device for making house prices go up, fuelled by poor people.

The system works until the supply of poor people starts to run out – until the torrent of poor people flowing into the machine slows down and becomes a trickle.

The system works until you realise that it was the power of the torrent that was driving the rise in house prices.

A few people understood what would happen when the torrent became a trickle. One of these people was Nassim Taleb, the future author of *The Black Swan*. Taleb, who knew the trick of making millions, understood a simple fact: as soon as the torrent slowed down, house prices would level off.

And if house prices levelled off, a big part of the banking system, fuelled by those rising house prices, would grind to a halt. And if a big part of the banking system ground to a halt, there would be a huge financial crash.

Taleb, who ran a hedge fund, saw an opportunity. He bet against the banking system. He bet on a future financial crash.

Then the torrent slowed.

Then house prices did level off.

Then millions of poor people – who needed their houses to rise in value in order to pay their mortgages – failed to pay their mortgages.

Then all the hedge funds and the finance companies and the investment banks, who had bought the CDOs, which they relied on for an income stream, were suddenly left empty-handed.

So when Matt's Rock asked the hedge funds and the finance companies and the investment banks for the usual short-term loan, so they could keep Matt's just-in-time machine going, the funds and the companies and the banks did not say their usual cheerful 'yes'.

They said sorry.

They said no.

Which meant that the Rock's just-in-time-machine ground to a halt.

It was August 2007. Matt's Rock went into freefall.

Down and down it went, into a deep black hole, burning money as it fell.

Along with other banks, Matt's Rock had made bets, and lost those bets, and made more bets, and lost those bets, too. In the end, the Bank of England lent the Rock some money to pay for the damage.

The amount was an eleven-figure sum.

Around this time, Matt had an idea for a book. He would call it *The Rational Optimist.*

***

I arrange to meet Matt for tea in a patisserie near the Ritz Hotel in London.

On the way I think about what it must have been like to be Matt when his bank went down. The anxious weeks of clinging on. The spread shrinking. The spread shrinking to nothing. The spread shrinking to less than nothing. The spread going into reverse. The Rock bleeding money.

Then, in April, the warning from the Bank of England: 'participants can be hit by sharp reductions in market liquidity'.

May and June. Still clinging on. July. Still clinging on, but only just. Then the American CDOs go bad. Then the hedge funds and finance companies and investment banks start to bleed money. The Rock needs a loan! Just to tide it over!

But the Rock can't get a loan.

Now Matt is desperate. The Rock asks the Bank of England for a loan. And somehow ... how did this happen ... how on earth ... but it does.

The news gets out.

The Rock's in trouble, and the news leaks. The news is that the Rock needs help. The news is that the Rock needs a shoulder to cry on. The news is that the Rock's got problems. Issues. A dependency. The Rock's got a habit. The Rock needs to go to rehab.

But if you're a bank, that's the one thing that can't happen. Banking is all about confidence. If you're a bank, you can't ever admit you're in trouble. You can't admit fear. You can't admit weakness. If you're a bank, you must be strong. You must be firm – a rock, in fact. But, in August 2007, the Rock is not a rock. In 2007, the Rock needs help.

And this all gets *out* ... there's a news item on the TV. The Rock's going *down*. And maybe it wasn't going down. But now it is. People are watching the TV. The reporter is Robert Peston. The Rock needs help. That's what Peston says. And thousands of people, the Rock's customers, have the exact same idea at the exact same time. The idea is: get to the nearest branch as soon as possible. Then withdraw every penny. And they do. It's the first run on a British bank for 130 years.

And it's all on TV.

So now the Rock is bleeding money from every orifice.

Millions! Tens of millions!

Imagine being Matt. But that's not the worst of it. He must answer to a parliamentary select committee. It's like being on trial. Matt arrives at his trial in a black suit. White shirt. Navy blue tie. Almost, but not quite, dressed for his own funeral. He is bespectacled and balding. He sits at the desk. He displays the body language of shame. Head pointing slightly down. Like a man on a ledge, looking into the abyss.

Hundreds of millions!

The inquisitor is John McFall. Grey fox. Hair greased back. Glaswegian. He lashes Matt over a number of exchanges.

He says: 'Were you aware of the Bank of England's report?'

And later: 'What did you do?'

And later: 'I would suggest to you, Dr Ridley, you failed.'

And later: 'You did not take corrective action that was successful.'

And later: 'The Bank of England's warning.'

And later: 'Sharp reductions in market liquidity.'

And later: 'Now that was in April.'

And later: 'So, what you did, from April until the tenth of August, seemed to have no effect whatsoever on the position that you found yourself in.'

Matt talks. He stammers a few words. McFall says: 'Dr Ridley, let's forget about the words here.'

And later: 'You're telling us this was unpredicted. But this was informed to you by the Bank of England in April.'

And later: 'You were warned.'

Matt gets the words out: 'We were not warned of a complete freezing of all global liquidity markets.'

McFall is not finished. He says: 'Listen. Let me just read it to you again.'

Matt sits on the ledge. What could he possibly say? That swapping is good. That money helps you swap, therefore money is good. That exchange, powered by money, encourages specialisation, and that specialisation encourages innovation, and that innovation encourages exchange, an auto-catalytic process, a nuclear reaction of sorts, and this nuclear reaction has made us rich beyond the craziest ambitions of our ancestors. Not because politicians have arranged for this to happen. But because somewhere, 15,000 years ago, a talented fisherman saw a chance to improve his situation. And then people started trading, which forced them to trust each other, and it wasn't long before we had money, and then banking, and now banks help people trade important things, like houses, by lending them money. But it's not all plain sailing, Mr McFall. Imagine, if you will, building a just-in-time machine for buying and selling money simultaneously in the here-and-now and in an imagined future. This is a machine that relies, for its fuel, on short-term loans from hedge funds and investment banks. A machine that works perfectly, thanks to precisely calibrated financial engineering, and that would grind to a halt in one circumstance and one circumstance only – namely the complete freezing of global liquidity markets. And how many times, Mr McFall, has that ever happened in our lifetime? *Once.*

But Matt says none of this. Matt listens. McFall continues to lash him. Matt looks sick. A few days later, he jumps off the ledge. He resigns as the Chairman of Northern Rock.

After he jumps, Matt starts to write *The Rational Optimist*. As a fan of Matt's writing, I buy the book as soon as I can and read it in two days. I find it scintillating – it creates sparks in the mind.

Do I think Matt's thesis is right – that, if you're rational, you must be optimistic about the future of the human race?

I *want* him to be right.

But one thing bothers me. I need to ask him about one thing.

***

I walk into the patisserie. It's noisy. A waitress buzzes around holding a tray stacked with crockery. A coffee machine hisses like the *Flying Scotsman*. I'm holding my recording device. Matt is sitting towards the back. He's wearing an open-necked shirt and chinos. I sit down. It's such a nice day, says Matt – maybe we should go to the park and have some ice cream. But we decide to stay in the patisserie.

We order coffee.

Then I tell Matt what bothers me. 'Just one thing,' I say. I feel like Lieutenant Columbo.

Freeze the action for a moment. Press Pause. Matt is looking at me. I am beginning to raise my forefinger.

The thing that bothers me is this one particular aspect of exchange.

If you go back in history, deep in the ancestral past, we started to swap things, keeping a mental record of who owed what to whom. That's not what bothers me. That's great. That made us rich, because swapping created an explosion of innovation. Then we started to use money. That's not what bothers me either. Money is great, because money helps you swap. When you add money to swapping, something magic happens. Swapping things via the medium of money is much better than just swapping things, because the presence of money acts like an X-ray.

That's because when people swap objects for money, they make offers and bids *in money*, and then, at the exact moment of exchange, they agree on a price. And this agreement, this *quantification*, sets a whole chain of events in motion. The existence of a price tells you how valuable an object is *compared with money*, and also how valuable it is *compared with other objects*.

So money gives you prices. And prices tell you about other people. What they want. What they need. Prices are a calibration of what people actually think and feel. They radically change the nature of human interaction. We may not always see this, because we're so used to it. But imagine a world in which you could go on a date and see exactly how much the other person wanted to have sex with you – not just in the blurred language of eye contact and gesture, but in precise measurements. Imagine if you could look across the table and see the other person's *numbers*. People might get used to this, after a few centuries. But it would feel pretty radical at first.

But it's not the emergence of prices that bothers me – or 'price discovery', as economists say. Price discovery just means translating everything into money. It's where we live a lot of the time in our heads. An increasing amount of time.

My house is worth four Ferraris; my lunch is worth two movie tickets; I can fly to Barcelona for the price of a pair of jeans; a top footballer is worth the same as an Old Master painting.

And price discovery has another amazing quality. As we've seen, it creates markets – it makes us all into buyers and sellers. It helps us to see what we might sell, and shows us exactly what we can afford to buy. So it guides us, collectively, towards matching desire with fulfilment – or, as they say, demand with supply. It tells you that, if you want money, you must think about other people, and what will induce them to part with money – in other words, you must focus on what other people need. That's the first gravy train. The second gravy train is what they want. That comes later.

Another thing about price discovery – it doesn't just create markets. It creates *self-regulating* markets. Imagine a city where people drink a lot of juice. In Juice City, people like juice, and this encourages other people to sell juice. Lots of people sell juice in Juice City because lots of people like juice in Juice City, and this keeps the price of juice stable – let's say £1 per carton. If one juice seller tried to charge £2, people would just buy their juice from someone else.

Now let's say there's a flood in Juice City. The river bursts its banks. Every juice seller is flooded out. All the juice is spoiled. People are stranded in their upstairs bedrooms, with no juice to drink. But then someone has an idea. Mr Sharp lives a few miles from Juice City. He goes to the supermarket, buys 100 cartons of juice, rents a motor launch, and cruises around Juice City, selling juice to people through their bedroom windows. He discovers that people are thirsty – so thirsty they are prepared to pay £10 per carton of juice.

But what, exactly, is that £10? It's a signal. It says: people need juice in Juice City! It says: bring juice to Juice City and you'll make huge profits! It encourages people to sell juice where juice is needed, if only to make profits for themselves.

Of course, the second wave of juice sellers don't make quite as much profit as Mr Sharp. With more sellers in the market, they must put their prices down. So the price of juice goes down – to £8, then £5, then £4.

That's why price discovery doesn't bother me. Even nakedly exploitative markets, like Juice City – actually New Orleans in the aftermath of Hurricane Katrina – are self-regulating. Demand pushes prices up; high prices bring new sellers to the market; prices go down. Demand attracts supply via the medium of money.

Swapping is good. Swapping things for money is good. Money helps you swap. Therefore money is good.

None of this bothers me.

What bothers me is what happens when people swap money for money. That's because when people swap one type of money for another type of money – when they trade in currency or financial products such as stocks and bonds – markets are not self-regulating. They are volatile. They are dangerous and crazy.

They are subject to bubbles and crashes.

When people trade in money, they turn hot-blooded. Like climbers within sight of the summit, they see only opportunity. They become like Joe Simpson on Siula Grande. They become like Matt's Rock.

And then, without warning, they get spooked. Joined to the ice cliff by the points of their ice axes and the spikes on the front of their shoes, they look down at the abyss below, and see only danger. Suddenly, without warning, they turn thin-blooded.

There's something weird about money. It can heat the blood. It can thin the blood. We can't control ourselves around it. It intoxicates us.

It intoxicates banks. They see bets they think they can't lose. Intoxicated banks borrow more money so they can bet more money. They create bubbles and crashes. Central banks spawn yet more money to pay for the crashes. The bubbles are getting bigger. The crashes are getting bigger.

Money is being spawned at an alarming rate. We still have faith in it. We still believe in the dance of specialisation and innovation, even when it comes to money.

Somewhere in our minds, we believe the secret of prosperity is our ability to spawn money.

But one day, a crash will be too big. To pay for it, central banks will spawn too much money.

And very quickly, we will lose our faith.

We will no longer believe.

That's what bothers me.

Go back 300 years, to the dawn of modern finance. The first proper insurance company, Lloyds of London, moved into office premises in 1691. The first central bank, the Bank of England, was formed in 1694. The first government bonds were issued in 1694. The London Stock Exchange started in 1698.

Things happened quickly. People started to get rich quickly. There were bubbles. But there were crashes.

Imagine the global economy as a dog. The dog represents people swapping things. The tail represents people swapping money – in other words, modern finance.

The dog is stable. The tail is volatile.

Still, the tail is in proportion to the dog.

Look at the economy now. The dog is much bigger. But the significant difference is the tail. The tail has grown relative to the dog. The tail has grown out of all proportion. Now the tail is much bigger than the dog.

The tail is volatile.

The tail controls us. It controls the way we think. It has colonised our minds.

That's what bothers me.

OK. Now press Play.

I look at Matt. I raise my forefinger. I don't mention the dog. But I tell him a short version of what bothers me.

'I'm glad you pointed that out,' says Matt.

He tells me he agrees with me – that he, too, had 'a moment on the road to Damascus. I can remember the penny dropping.'

The penny dropped for Matt after he resigned from the Rock. He was listening to a talk by the Nobel laureate Vernon Smith.

Smith, an economist who has worked at Stanford and the California Institute of Technology, won his Nobel prize for devising a series of experiments in which people trade different types of things. He discovered that when people trade money or assets, markets are not stable. But when people trade 'hamburgers or haircuts' – or massages, cake, orange juice or coffee – markets are stable.

Matt says, 'The process that got the coffee from the Brazilian field to this cup works unbelievably well.'

He says, 'On the whole, the best thing to do to that kind of market is to leave it alone, and let it sort things out. It's unbelievably good at innovating, it's unbelievably good at driving down the cost of things.'

He's talking about markets for goods and services – the dog, rather than the tail.

He says: 'Over the long term, it's unbelievable how much cheaper things have got.'

This is one of the main points in *The Rational Optimist* – that, over the last few centuries, almost everything has been getting cheaper in real terms – or, to look at it another way, if we want something, we need to spend less and less time working in order to pay for it.

'Prosperity,' Matt writes, 'is simply saved time.'

Now, he looks at me and says: 'This is my electric lighting example.'

In *The Rational Optimist*, Matt gives lots of examples of things that are getting better. People in Botswana are richer now than Scandinavians were in the middle of the last century. The Chinese are 'ten times as rich' as they were in 1955 – and their life expectancy has increased by twenty-eight years. Half a century ago, prosperous people in rich countries had flush toilets, telephones, washing machines, fridges and TV sets. Now almost everyone has these things, even the very poor – even unemployed people on benefits.

All because of the dog. The dog brings forth innovation, efficiency and saved time – time for clear thinking, time to invent tools.

And the best example of the dog is electric light.

In *The Rational Optimist*, Matt asks how much time you'd need to work to buy an hour of artificial light. In Babylonian times, in the age of oil lamps, you'd have to work for fifty hours for an hour of light. Artificial light was strictly for the rich. In 1800, in the age of tallow candles, you'd have to work for six hours. In 1880, when the kerosene lamp was invented, you'd have to work for fifteen minutes. In 1950: eight seconds. Now: half a second.

That's the dog. I have no problem with the dog. For me, the problem is the *tail*. Because the tail – the volatile tail, the tail that intoxicates us and makes us hot-blooded and thin-blooded – is now wagging the dog. I'm not an economist. But that's my strong feeling. That's why the economy crashed, and will crash again.

And the crashes are getting bigger and bigger.

The tail is wagging the dog.

Now Matt talks about the tail. 'The history of finance and asset markets – tulips, jewels, railway stocks, everything – is bedevilled by booms and busts. You constantly get bubbles … since 1720, we've been figuring out how to …'

He pauses for a moment, during which time his mind zooms back to the dawn of modern finance, and alights on the South Sea Bubble, its first big consequence.

People bought South Sea shares, which made prices go up, which made people buy more shares, which made prices go up even more, which made people buy more shares … and then people started to sell their shares, which made prices go down, which made people sell more, which made prices go down even more.

People climbed. They got summit fever. Then they looked down. They saw the abyss.

The bubble was followed by a crash.

'There's a lovely bit in Macaulay,' says Matt, 'where he says, the parliament that met in perplexity after the crash, after the South Sea Bubble in 1720, would be *astonished* at the prosperity we now have. He's writing 110 years later. He's saying everybody thinks we had this terrible collapse … A few years later it's back again.'

In other words: there are bubbles and crashes. But over time, the wealth comes back, and we move on. The general trend is upwards. We swap, we invent, we light up our rooms and our lives.

'Now,' says Matt, 'how you run asset markets in such a way that you don't get bubbles, I don't know.'

He says: 'I'm quite careful not to go too much on the record about my own experience with Northern Rock, but we were worried about credit risk rather than liquidity risk.'

Matt was worried about the solvency of the people the Rock lent money to, rather than the solvency of the other banks they borrowed money from.

'It should have been the other way round,' he says.

Then he says: 'The reason we were worried about that was very much because it was the signal we were getting from our regulator and the Bank of England.'

And: 'Both of them were saying: credit risk was the thing to worry about.'

And: 'If you have twice-yearly sessions with the person from the Financial Services Authority, and they don't use the words "liquidity risk", and they go on and on about credit risk …'

And: 'You can't help but be steered.'

The Rock was steered. It crashed.

But still. Here we are. Drinking coffee in a patisserie next to the Ritz Hotel. The process that got the coffee from a Brazilian field to our cups worked unbelievably well.

And anyway, where do you draw the line? You can't imagine a world without modern finance – without loans, or stock markets, or derivatives. There will be bubbles and crashes. We must deal with them. Vernon Smith believes that people who have experienced bubbles and crashes get better at dealing with them. They learn to be less hot-blooded during the bubble and less thin-blooded during the crash.

'In the end,' says Matt, 'I say to myself, well, you go back to 1830 and you tell someone, no, you can't borrow money to build a railway. That's stupid – it would be great to borrow money to build a railway, because you'll get it all back. And so the answer must be: borrowing from posterity, which is what we're doing – borrowing from our children – can still be a good thing. If we invest the money *wisely*.'

I feel momentarily light-headed.

I say: 'If it … enables you to create more time!'

My brain performs a calculation.

I say: 'You're taking time *away* from your grandchildren. But hell, you might be *repaying* them with yet more time!'

Matt says: 'Exactly!'

Then he says: 'And this is the staggering … the *staggering* prosperity of posterity if things continue as they are.'

He considers this for a moment. 'They can afford to pay this gigantic debt out of petty cash.'

We talk on. I love Matt. He's terribly charming. There are several things I envy in him: his clarity of thought, his erudition, the fact that he finished his Ph.D, which was on the mating habits of pheasants.

For a while we discuss the mating habits of humans. He says something fascinating about sex, and it gives me an idea.

I make a mental note.

A hot day. An upmarket patisserie. I order more coffee. Matt orders ice cream. We carry on talking.

The waitress drops a tray. There's an explosion of smashing crockery, followed by a moment of silence.

***

Joe Simpson was hanging off the side of a mountain, in a blizzard, with a badly broken leg, looking into a crevasse. His climbing partner, Simon Yates, was higher up the mountain, holding the rope.

Joe's weight was pulling Simon off the mountain.

Simon made a calculation.

Sitting at the kitchen table in his thick-walled Yorkshire cottage, Joe says: 'Think of it this way. It was a no-brainer. Simon didn't know whether I was one foot off the ground, almost touching the ground. Maybe I was fifteen feet off the deck. Maybe I was fifty feet off the deck. But fifty feet off a steep ice slope is survivable. Ski-jumpers survive, right?'

We are drinking tea. Joe says: 'All he knew was he was 300 feet off the deck. It's a no-brainer! He was going to die. And he's not going to die and find, in the process of dying, I only fell one foot.'

Joe pauses. 'So. He cut the rope.'

Joe fell. He has said it felt like a dream. He has said it felt fast, yet endless; that he watched himself from above; that the fall itself wasn't frightening.

He fell fifty feet, and hit a plug of snow at the top of the crevasse, and fell fifty feet more through the snow, and smashed against something, his fall broken by the snow, and he couldn't breathe, and then he could. He was in the crevasse. On a ledge.

He spent the night on the ledge. His situation was gradually becoming clear. There were shards of hope. Maybe Simon would find him in the morning. Maybe he would be able to climb from the ledge to the top of the crevasse. He tried. But he couldn't. The wall of the crevasse was icy and overhanging.

'I got a couple of feet and fell back down. My leg was completely bollocksed. I don't think I could have done it with two good legs,' Joe says.

When Rick gave *Touching the Void* to Callum, and Callum gave it to me, and I read about the climb – the skyscraper of ice, the accident, the crevasse, the ledge – I saw it as a story about one man's personal hell.

A man who tried to climb too high. A tragedy.

But it wasn't a tragedy. Joe survived. He wrote a book. The book was made into a film. Since the great success of the book, and particularly since the film, Joe has given hundreds of motivational talks. He makes £10,000 or £15,000 per talk. For a while, he gave a talk every week.

The talks are about falling into a crevasse.

But also something else.

'It was just the most bleak point I've ever been in my life,' says Joe. 'I was absolutely scared stupid, because I had to assess where I was. Now, Simon hadn't found me by nine o'clock in the morning. He would've found me by then. So he was either dead, or he thought I was dead. So if he thought I was dead, he'd have gone down.'

Joe was stuck on the ledge. He couldn't climb up. He couldn't go sideways. 'And, if I stayed where I was, I was going to die. You don't die of a broken leg. You die very slowly of hypothermia and dehydration.'

Joe says: 'I had a good sleeping bag, which I'd get into. I'd eat a shit-load of snow. And I'd die. Very slowly, in a twilight world. It was just ... it was a horrible nightmare. Crevasses are nightmarishly claustrophobic places to be. If you're on your own in them. A bit of a tomb-y feeling to them. The feel of a tomb. Closed in. And I'd had a very distressing night, screaming Simon's name, listening to it echoing around.'

Joe says: 'Up I couldn't do. Sideways I couldn't do. Staying where I was, I couldn't do. The only thing was going deeper ... and so I did it. But it scared the fuck out of me. Because it was completely counter-intuitive. You know, if you're buried alive, you don't dig yourself deeper, and that's what I was doing.'

He thinks for a moment. 'And yet I just thought, I partly thought, if there's nothing down there, I'll die quickly.'

Joe's talks are about falling into a crevasse. But also something else. They're about what he learned when he fell into a crevasse. He needed to take the hard choice. So he did. He couldn't live on the ledge. So he dropped into the void.

We know what happened. Fifty feet below the ledge, he found himself in a vast subterranean dome, 'as big as St Paul's Cathedral'. At the bottom of this dome, where the walls narrowed again, was a wedge of snow.

The crevasse had a false floor.

Underneath the false floor was a chasm – certain death. But the false floor led to a cone of ice. The cone of ice led to the surface.

Joe inched along the false floor. It crackled and crunched. Bits kept falling into the chasm. But Joe got to the other side. He climbed the cone of ice.

Joe was hot-blooded. He saw risks as opportunities. He made mistakes. He corrected his mistakes. He lived to tell the tale. 'I discovered I could write,' he says, 'which I never would have done. And so it gave me a career. It led to me becoming a speaker.'

After the financial crisis, many of his talks were to banks. He names two: 'HSBC. Deutsche Bank.'

The banks tried to climb too high. They fell into a crevasse. Now they need to make hard choices.

They pay £15,000 to listen to Joe's talk.

'They find it inspiring,' Joe says. 'God knows why.'

4

Something is wrong, and I don't know what it is. Or rather, I do know what it is, but I don't know how it works.

The mechanism. I don't know how it works.

I need to know how it works.

Tomorrow I'm going to see the Russian. I'm trying to understand what motivates the Russian. I'm trying to imagine what it's like to *be* him. He did not have my advantages. He grew up in an apartment block in Leningrad. He defected to the West at the age of eighteen. Very early in life, he bolted towards the West – towards free exchange, specialisation, winner-take-all. He had focus. Clarity of thought.

He knew how the West worked. We native Westerners mostly don't. We don't see the lines of power and exploitation. We like to delude ourselves. We're experts in self-delusion.

The Russian, whose name was Leonid Maxovich Rodovinsky, went to America and changed his name to Leon Max.

Leon Max did not delude himself. He made more than half a billion dollars.

I'm in my house, feeling jumpy, thinking about Leon Max.

I try to make myself a cup of coffee. I arrange the coffee grounds, the cafetiere, the spoonful of honey. Then the boiling water. My phone is switched off. People call and text me because I owe them money. They send me emails. They send me letters. Then I put the letters on the kitchen table.

Sometimes I open the letters. I look at the wording. We will come and take things from you; we can come and break your door down and take your things and sell your things at auctions.

They will break my door. They will take my things.

My things. I have very few valuable things. I have a work by the artist David Hockney which he gave me when I interviewed him in his lovely house in the Hollywood Hills. That's about all I have. Later, I interviewed Damien Hirst in *his* lovely house on the north Devon coast. Now there's a guy who understands how to get people's attention. I asked him to draw something for me.

He drew a penis on a post-it note. And the thing is, I don't know where this post-it note is. I think it might be in my garage, in a box, one of perhaps a hundred boxes of clutter in my garage. When they come for me, when they break down my door, I will take them to my garage, and make them wait while I go through the boxes. Here, I will say finally. Here it is. A penis. Drawn on a post-it note by the richest artist in the world. Take that to the auction. Take that, and wait for the bids to come in. And then bring me the change.

The coffee is still in the cafetiere. Now it's too cold to drink. It's a hot day. My coffee is too cold, and also too warm.

Something is wrong. Something is not working properly. I want to be rich, but I don't want to be rich; a demon in my head is making me want to be poor, and I don't understand how the demon works, and I want to understand how the demon works, I want to find the demon and tell it to stop.

I know exactly how to get rich. All the components are there. These components, they're all in my mind; I just need to piece them together, to join them up. I just need to make one big effort to join up the pieces. Focus on the task. Focus! I can do it. I can do it if I want to do it.

If somebody said, make millions, if they said you have to make a given number of millions over the next three years – these are people who have captured me, and the choice they are offering me is to make millions or to be buried alive, in a coffin, six feet underground, and left to die a slow, contemplative death – I'd say, sure I can make the given number of millions, and I would.

Or they could say, we will drug you and when you wake up, you will be on a ledge on a cliff of ice 2,000 feet above the ground, with another 2,000 feet of ice above you. Damn! Then I would make the given number of millions.

I would. I could. The components are there.

For instance, I'm not a socialist. I'm not one of those people who wants to tax and squeeze the rich; I'm mostly on the other side of that argument. You have to ask yourself: what is the optimum amount to tax people? Well, it's not zero, obviously. And it's not 100 per cent – that's equally obvious. It's not 90 per cent. It's not 80 per cent. Not 70, or 60, or 50. You don't want to ruin people, or chase them away.

When I made a lot more money, I would never have admitted this, but I had a gut feeling the whole system was unfair. Sure, when you make more money, you have to pay more tax – I got that. But should you have to pay a bigger *proportion* of your money, just because you've had a good year?

Let's think about this. At first, way back, everybody had to pay the exact same amount. Then, later, you had to pay the same proportion – a tithe. These days, the proportion gets bigger as you make more money. How did rich people ever let that happen? I guess because they don't really pay the tax – they only pretend to pay it.

And when people talk about the rich in that particular tone, like they hate the rich, they want to destroy the rich, or at least take their money, I'm the guy who says, what do you think the rich actually *do* with their money? And people say: they spend it on yachts. That's what they always say. The bright white boats in the bright blue water, with beautiful women in swimsuits jumping into the water and then climbing back on the boat and maybe smoking a cigarette. The rich love the water. I used to wonder why. Why do they love being wet, the rich? Actually, they don't love being wet. They love being *dry*. That's why they love the water, the rich. Because they love being dry, and if you want to do something, like smoke a cigarette or go to bed or drink a cup of coffee, it's much more expensive to do any of these things around water, because you need to spend a lot of money on whatever it is that's keeping you dry – in this case, the yacht. It's actually not very comfortable on a yacht. It's OK when the yacht is moving – cutting through the water in that way that makes the front slightly stick up. That feels exhilarating. But otherwise – no. It feels like you're in a small house, and the house is slipping around under your feet.

But aside from yachts, what do the rich really do with their money? That's the question I ask. Of course, they spend it on expensive houses, like Felix Dennis and Leon Max – and Jordan Belfort, before he went to jail. But mostly, they invest it. In other words, they lend money to people who have good business ideas. Being rich, they tend to be good at spotting good business ideas. They're funding the economy, is what they're doing. And what would happen if you took their money and gave it to politicians? Well, those politicians would invest the money too. Being politicians, they are not very good at spotting good business ideas. Being politicians, they are very good at spotting business ideas that will appeal to the specific type of voter they're trying to impress. If you give politicians money, they will use it to impress voters – but, in the end, they will waste it.

I'm not sure I believe all of this. But I believe some of it. Who would you put in charge of the money? Rich people – or bossy people? The answer is not obvious to me. In any case, there's something fishy about the whole idea of tax in any modern economy. When governments want money, they just need to print it. But printing money causes inflation (or rather, it *is* inflation). Inflation causes prices to rise, and this can easily spiral out of control, which terrifies governments. So they tax people to reduce their spending power, in order to stop the inflationary death spiral they're so scared of. That's really what tax is for. Which means, actually, that it makes sense to tax rich people *less* than the rest of us, because there aren't very many of them, so their spending habits don't push prices up very much. A rich person makes fifty times more money than a normal person, but he doesn't eat fifty breakfasts or drive fifty cars. He buys one or two Rolls-Royces, and a Mercedes for his chauffeur.

Sure, he pushes up the price of Rolls-Royces. And German cars. And yachts. And those seats on planes that fold down into beds. Do I actually believe this?

In any case, the problem is not my politics.

My education, then? Thinking about my education, trying to sum it up in a single picture, I see lawns, trees, courtyards, quadrangles, old buildings and ancient buildings and gleaming white modern buildings and green spaces and rich kids, quite rich kids, very rich kids. A picture jumps into my mind of the last student accommodation I lived in – the big room, the swimming pool, the rich kids next door, gold Rolls parked outside.

An outlier. Not typical. But still. I was at school with rich kids. I was poorer than most of them – more than half, I'm sure, probably more than three-quarters. I didn't usually feel poor. But sometimes – yes, I did. I remember one boy, he really was poor, or poor-ish, he'd got some kind of scholarship, and he was bawling me out one day in the dormitory, I was eleven, and he ended his tirade with: 'just because your parents have money!' And I felt proud, was glad that others were around and had heard; money was precisely what I worried my parents did not have, or at least did not have in great amounts. My father was a psychologist, and did something connected to the United Nations I didn't understand. He wasn't around much. He had an apartment in Germany, and then one in Holland, and spent time in the Third World and communist eastern Europe. Then he bought a very 1970s house in the middle of a forest in Nova Scotia. He kept disappearing, my father. My mother used to say he wasn't interested in making money – not at all, in fact. His ideal was to live as if money didn't exist.

I have a memory of my mother saying: 'They asked him how much he wanted – and he said, just pay me what you think I'm worth!'

Slight incredulity in her tone of voice. She sort of admired my father's attitude. But she also sort of wished he'd asked for more money.

One day I went on a sponsored walk with some kids from my school. We walked along the Sussex Downs. I realised we were going to walk past a place where you could see my parents' house, or rather one of their houses, in the distance. They were not living there at the time. They weren't even renting it out. It was empty. But there it was. It looked small and ordinary. I felt this desperate urge to point it out, even though I knew I shouldn't, that this would be asking for trouble. But I did anyway. And this other kid started laughing at me. 'That's your parents' house? Hey! That's Leith's parents' house!' A few kids looked. Most were not interested. I wanted to say, for fuck's sake! My parents have three houses! And one of them has two balconies and a sunken living room and a fireplace made from lumps of granite the size of television sets! All true. But I did not say these things.

A bit further along, the kid pointed at a shed. 'That's Leith's house,' he said.

At school, I studied literature in Latin, French and English, and learned the German language. I read and re-read works by Catullus, Pliny, Voltaire, Molière, Camus, Anouilh, Shakespeare, Marlowe, Milton, Chaucer, Austen, Hardy, Dickens, Keats, Wordsworth and Larkin. In maths, I got stuck after calculating the gradient of a curve. I could calculate the gradient of a curve. But that was it. Anything beyond that, I was stuck. Then I forgot how to calculate the gradient of a curve. Something about numbers disturbed me; they were capable of making sudden jumps and then they'd nail you, and you'd be sitting there, helpless, while they went on nailing you.

I was sent to maths tutors. I had three – a blond-haired man, a dark-haired man and a diabetic woman who lived in Rottingdean and who would go droopy and hazy and who once passed out in front of me. She was my last hope. I had failed and failed; I needed to pass an exam to get anywhere. She found the key to my problem. She showed me how to control the numbers. They are automata. They do what they are told. You need to order them around. They will obey. I passed the exam. I decided to put numbers behind me. To forget the whole thing. A bad idea.

My housemaster arranged a trip to an investment bank in the City of London. Bankers took us aside and tried to explain how they made money. It seemed too simple. You bought things when you thought they'd get more expensive, and you sold them when you thought they'd get cheaper. You had to develop a grasp of the processes that made these things change in value. The things were financial products – money dressed up in different costumes. You swapped one type for another type, which was like making a bet. With experience, you could win more often than you lost. You could also get good at calculating how much money to risk on each bet. A couple of boys sat there, and their eyes lit up. But the place felt gloomy to me; it provoked my anxiety. I felt trapped. These guys were wearing jackets and ties, just like school uniform. I wondered why. They were rich; they could have worn anything they wanted.

We had been drinking filter coffee, I'd had a few cups, and I needed to piss, was desperate to piss, and I kept on putting it off. I don't know why. When I finally went, the housemaster followed me in, and pissed into the urinal next to mine. He unzipped, and his piss gushed into the ceramic bowl. My bladder froze. I could not piss. I was desperate to piss, but could not. I zipped up, and washed my hands, and walked back across the trading floor.

All these years later I'm sitting in my house, thinking about Leon Max. The Russian, is how I think of him. The Russian had no delusions. The Russian did not fear numbers. The Russian lives in Easton Neston, which might be the finest example of what's known as the English Country House. Architectural critics rave about this place. It's almost perfect. People think the original drawings were made by Christopher Wren, the most famous architect in history. But at some point in the 1690s, for some reason, Wren passed the project to his assistant Nicholas Hawksmoor. It was Hawksmoor's first country house. He really let himself go. Look at a picture of Easton Neston. Clean lines. Lots of big windows. A sense of order and contained power. Classier than Buckingham Palace or the White House.

There's something about this house, something I can't place, that affects me viscerally, a drip of anxiety in my gut.

***

124

In the morning I realise what it is. I walk around my own house, pondering what it is about Max's house that gives me a drip of anxiety in my gut. My house is fine, by the way. My house is not a problem. It's a modern house in a complex of identical modern houses. It's a condominium. In *Breaking Bad*, when Walter White splits up with his wife, he moves into a condominium. My house is like that. It's a perfect house for people to live in when they are getting divorced. Three bedrooms. Open-plan ground floor. Nine hundred and fifty square feet. On a yacht, only a billionaire would have this much space.

The Russian's house gives me a drip of anxiety in my gut because it reminds me of a building I used to know when I was a student. The same pale stone, the same sense of order and contained power. It makes me think of being frantic and desperate, racking my brains, trying to think of something. Walking fast, late for a tutorial, unprepared, turning into an avenue of ancient trees, very tall trees, and there is the building, the pale stone structure visible through the trees.

I remember walking between the trees, towards the building, racking my brains. Trying to think of something. But no. It would not come.

I was studying philosophy. I was a graduate student. The thing that wouldn't come was an idea for my dissertation, which would, I hoped, be the foundation of my thesis. But I couldn't decide what to write about. It needed to be about my philosophy. Well, yes. But I had not yet worked out what my philosophy was, beyond the fact that it bordered on nihilism.

What could anybody really know? And even if you did know something, how would you know you knew it? That was my philosophy.

Consider this. What is a fact? A fact is something you know. Well, not quite. The word is derived from the Latin *facere* – to make. A fact is something you make. A fact is something you make *up*. In other words, a fact is really a fiction. Now look at the world. Observe it. Does it exhibit regularities? Does it abide by rules? And how do we understand these rules? By observing facts. In other words, by creating fictions.

Imagine you're a chicken. That's what Bertrand Russell said. Every day, you wake up hungry. Every day, the farmer feeds you. That's how your world works. It exhibits regularities. It abides by rules. The farmer wants to stop you being hungry. The farmer has your best interests at heart. That's what the facts tell you. The farmer feeds you every day, for 99 days. On the 100th day, you wake up hungry, as usual. The farmer opens the door of your coop. But he is not holding the usual handful of food. He's holding a shiny silver thing instead.

You observed the world. You saw fictions. You mistook them for facts. It's called the problem of induction.

And now you've been beheaded by the shiny silver thing, and you're running around without a head.

I had a sense that, metaphorically speaking, a shiny silver thing hung over my career as a scholar. I was walking down the avenue of tall trees, trying to formulate the central idea for my dissertation. I was on my way to a tutorial. I was late. I had given the impression, the strong impression, that today, at last, I would reveal my central idea.

As a philosopher, nothing is possible. That was my idea. The more I thought about this idea, the more powerful it seemed to get. It had gripped me, and now it wouldn't let me go. Philosophy is impossible. I didn't *want* it to be impossible. I yearned for it not to be impossible. I wanted to wake up one day, and find that the world had changed, and now philosophy was possible. That never happened.

Philosophy is about thinking clearly. It's about knowing what you can and cannot think. If you slip, if you make a mistake, if you think you know something when you don't, things can very quickly get out of control.

Also, philosophy is supposed to be about having thoughts that make the world a better place. It's an edifice you build. You build it by piling one clear thought on top of another. But what if you only have one clear thought? And what if that thought is that it's impossible to know, for certain, if any of your thoughts are clear?

In that case, you have two options. You can quit. Or you can cheat. You can build an edifice on thoughts that are not clear. The edifice will fall down. There will be consequences.

But maybe not for a while.

My tutorials all took place in this tiny yard that had been built in about 1350. It was actually occupied during the Peasants' Revolt. I'd go into this yard, and up a cold stone staircase, and knock on the thick oak door leading to my supervisor's rooms, and I believed that this was the set of rooms where Christopher Marlowe had gone when he was being grilled by his supervisor, in 1584 or whatever. He, too, would have climbed the stairs and said to himself: 'God, this place is old.' In his play *Doctor Faustus*, which I'd read over and over at school, he makes a powerful point about crossing over to the dark side. His point is: if you take one step, you're doomed. Not exactly because you won't be able to cover your tracks, but because you will no longer be the same person. When you take that step, it's already too late – you've already turned into somebody else.

I used to imagine Marlowe's mind would be occupied by this type of thought as he climbed the cold stone staircase and walked towards the thick oak door. But of course, it probably wasn't. He was probably fretting about the Ancients – Aristotle or Plato, or maybe, I don't know, Galen, or St Paul.

I walked down the avenue of tall trees. I was thinking of facts, and the fact that I believed facts were a fiction – the *fiction* that I believed facts were a fiction. The fiction that I believed *fictions* were …

The shiny thing was moving closer to my scholastic neck. I'd recently had an offer, not uninteresting, to try out as a journalist on a newspaper. I'd let it slide. Maybe I shouldn't have let it slide. Maybe I'd have to resurrect it. Maybe it was too late. Probably it was too late.

Journalism. Not really the same thing as philosophy.

At the end of the avenue of trees is a bridge. I walked towards the bridge. There was pressure in my head and a cold drip of anxiety in my stomach.

I stopped at the bridge and looked up at the building. Then I crossed the bridge, and for a moment the building blocked my view of the sky. I went through a gate and turned into a courtyard, and now I was on the other side of the building.

The building is the Wren Library. Built in the early 1690s. Designed by Christopher Wren. Brought to completion in about 1692 with the help of his assistant, Nicholas Hawksmoor.

When Wren was designing the library, and then building it with the help of Hawksmoor, in the 1680s and the early 1690s, something else was happening, something that would change the world for ever, and Wren was central to this change. In the past lay the Dark Ages, the world of superstition, necromancy, incantations and alchemy, a world in which men looked for answers in the old books, because they believed the Ancients knew more than they did, so they sat in their cold stone rooms, in the flickering candlelight, reading the same books over and over.

Things started to change when Galileo built a telescope and saw, with his own eyes, that the old books were wrong.

The Earth goes around the Sun!

Galileo was arrested and locked up, but that didn't finish him, he carried on, and curious men all over Europe began to doubt the old books – Francis Bacon, for instance, and William Harvey, who tied dogs to a table in his basement and cut into their arteries, noting that the dogs' blood spurted all over the walls, rather than just oozing out, which is what it said in the old books. Galen thought it would ooze. But no: it spurted.

Anyway, the psychopathically curious Harvey taught Charles Scarburgh, who taught Christopher Wren. Wren, who himself operated on dogs, and also designed sundials and telescopes, was one of the most curious of the curious men. Isaac Newton, whose rooms were in the next-but-one courtyard to the Wren Library, was another. Newton used to poke things in his *own eye* to find out how it worked. Wren and Newton both knew Robert Hooke, who built microscopes – another curious man. Edmund Halley, famous for noticing the comet that would be named after him, was yet another.

Once they saw that the old books were wrong, these men became fanatical. What they understood, what drove them, was precisely *the extent of their own ignorance* – they saw that the set of things they didn't know, but might know in the future, was far greater than the set of things they already knew. And this made them wildly optimistic.

It gave them a new concept – the concept of human progress.

***

On the way to see the Russian, I hook up with the photographer who will take pictures of the Russian and his house.

It's a bright, sunny day.

The photographer has a big black Audi, and I sit back and look up at the bright sky, thinking about the Russian, my mind also fizzing with half-formed ideas about Wren and Newton and Hooke and Halley, and all the rest of them. Boyle, of course, with his test tubes and beakers. All that glass! They started a society, the Royal Society, whose motto was *Nullius In Verba* – take nobody's word for it. See for yourself! Don't rely on the old books! They wanted to see, for themselves, how the world worked. They wanted to look at it, measure it, analyse it, quantify it, map it. Predict it. Turn it into numbers. Break it into pieces and watch the pieces interacting with each other, as if they were part of a machine. These guys *invented the scientific method* – they really did. They were actually doing it, actually inventing the scientific method, at the exact moment the Wren Library was being built.

The library, with its neoclassical order, its contained power, the whole beautiful artefact an insult to the problem of induction.

The library says: stop worrying about the problem of induction. You can take care of that later.

It says: look at the world. Trust your own eyes. Collect data.

It says: don't worry about being wrong. You're always wrong at the start. All knowledge is provisional. Just keep updating.

It says: you'll get there in the end.

It says: the world exhibits regularities.

It abides by rules.

It says: one day you will discover the rules. One day you will control the world.

The library *does not care* about the shiny thing in the farmer's hand.

This is what my mind is grappling with as the Audi swishes me through the countryside north of London. The seeking of facts. The power and influence of the scientific method. You try something one way, and then another way, until you think you see how it works. You build an edifice. Hooke observed mites and fleas through his microscope, and drew them with painstaking accuracy on the scale of rats. Harvey kept frogs, toads, cats and dogs in his basement. When he got home in the evening, he would go downstairs to do some vivisection. Then he would write notes.

Halley went to a town in Germany and collected records of everybody who lived and died there. He realised that, with enough data, he could construct a statistical analysis of people's lives. He could not know, for sure, how long a particular person would live. But he could calculate how long an *average* person would live.

The scientific method is about trying something one way, and then another way, to see how things work. It's about looking for regularities, and collecting data, and using this data to predict the future. It's about investing in the future. It inculcates the belief that the future is worth more than the past, because the value of the things you know is always smaller than the value of the things you are yet to discover.

That's the definition of progress. It's the secular religion of the modern age. It creates an economy that explodes outwards like a universe – an economy that works beautifully until it reaches the limits of nature. Progress does not recognise nature, because progress, as John Maynard Keynes showed us, exists in abstraction. It is based on data and the instruments, virtual and real, that data can make – insurance policies, loans, stocks, bonds, codes; looms, factories, mills, mines, iron bridges, viaducts, railways, power lines, pistons, engines, algorithms. Cars that purr like big cats.

The Audi cruises along the motorway, and turns into a local road, and finally into a narrow lane. Around the next corner, or the one after that, I'll get my first glimpse of the Russian's house.

I can see an avenue of trees.

And here it is – Easton Neston. A monument of controlled power rendered in pale stone. Big windows reflecting white light. I try to take it in.

The photographer walks up to the house and knocks on the door. Then he comes back. The Russian will be out in a few minutes. He will talk to me.

I walk up to the house and – wow. The facade is *right here*. The Wren wing is to my left. A courtyard lies beyond, and another, smaller courtyard beyond that. There is a wall to my right. Architecturally, the house is a cross between the Wren Library of my memory and the neoclassical ranges that flank it.

Standing here, I can feel the drip of anxiety in my gut.

And for a wormhole moment I'm back in time, looking up at the Wren Library, trying to find the words to describe my central idea, but the words will not come, I can't think clearly, and I walk beyond the courtyard, past Newton's rooms, past Francis Bacon's rooms, past William Harvey's rooms, past John Maynard Keynes' rooms, towards the tiny yard and up the cold stone steps, thinking that perhaps I can resurrect the offer from the newspaper, perhaps it's not too late.

Journalism. Not really the same thing as philosophy. I knock on the thick oak door.

Twenty-seven years later, I'm looking at the thick oak door of Easton Neston. It's the – what, exactly? The nicest house I've ever seen? Yes, quite the nicest house I have ever seen. Better than Francis Ford Coppola's, even though he did have a wraparound porch. Better than Robin Gibb's converted monastery. Better than Gordon Ramsay's chunky villa, better than Mike Stoller's vertiginous cliff-top eyrie, better than Damien Hirst's house on the north Devon coast, better than David Hockney's lovely house in the Hollywood Hills, decorated in the bright blue and green hues chosen by the artist himself. Better than the King of Lesotho's palace. Better than Dorsington!

Easton Neston. The nicest house in the world? It really might be. I have a strong sense of wanting it. I want it. But I wouldn't want to live here. I'd hate it. But I want it. But I'd hate it.

The door opens. It's the Russian.

***

He walks towards me across the gravel. He's small and well-dressed. White jeans and sandals. He looks very Russian.

We shake hands. A brief moment of intensity. Can I have some money? How much do you want? A million would do it. I'll get one of my people to transfer it immediately. The moment of intensity passes.

Leon Max made his money as a designer of women's clothes. The women in his ads are so feminine it's almost inhumane. High heels, narrow ankles, slender limbs, small high breasts, baby faces with adult cheekbones. He has dozens of retail outlets all over America and the Far East.

Max understands feminine allure. He gets the power it has. Not just over men. But over women. The need to exhibit, to advertise the self, to be loved. Max can sense the flow of oestrogen like a water diviner. He knows how to turn this flow, this river, into money.

We walk around the side of the house, which sits on a slight rise in the land. Behind the house is a reflecting pool, a series of sculpted box hedges, a lake, and an avenue of – elms? Or maybe limes? – marching into the distance until they join at the vanishing point.

'I want to live a beautiful life,' says Max, just after we have walked past the reflecting pool, which, from some angles, doubles the house's beauty. Later, he will tell me about his first wife: 'the most beautiful woman I have ever seen'. Beautiful house, beautiful wife. Also, he has beautiful feet. He's obviously had an expensive pedicure. He has the toenails of a man in his thirties. Or even twenties – they're not gnarled at all.

I look at the house, angled against the blue. I imagine Wren standing here, and Hawksmoor standing next to him, in this exact place, slightly more than three centuries ago, the house not yet real, but nevertheless doubled in the reflecting pool of their imaginations. Wren is holding the drawings. He's passing the project to Hawksmoor. The ambitious Wren has other things to do – St Paul's, certainly, but so much more. The world is changing fast, and Wren wants to be near its centre – London. The men of science and data have gripped the tiller. He sees himself as their focal point. His mind races with novelty and inventions. It's the 1690s – very soon, London will have a central bank, a proper stock exchange, and an insurance centre, Lloyds of London. Paper money will start to circulate. Money will increasingly flow towards people with ideas, rather than just those who already have it. The market will fizz with bubbles and crashes. The South Sea Bubble is a few years in the future. Parliament will meet in perplexity. Wealth will be created and destroyed and created again. The Industrial Revolution will give birth to the world of mechanical reproduction. Supply chains will circle the planet. The modern consumer will emerge. A German intellectual will take exception to the whole process; he will sit in the British Museum, day after day, preparing a counterbalancing tract. Half a century later, an exiled Russian will travel from Zurich to St Petersburg, and the city will soon take his name. Forty years after that, a boy will grow up in an apartment block in the city. At the age of eighteen, he will defect to America. He will dowse a vast, invisible current of oestrogen. He will make hundreds of millions of dollars. He will look for the most beautiful house in the world. He will find it.

'Well, Mr Hawksmoor,' says Wren, looking down from the slight rise in the land, 'will you do it?'

'Sir, it would be an honour.'

***

In the course of the next three hours, Max shows me around the house and grounds. He answers my questions. He was born in 1954. His father was a 'failed playwright'. His mother was a civil engineer. As a teenager, he had a part-time job stitching costumes for the Kirov Ballet. His sandals are by Prada, 'I think'. His suits are made in London and Hong Kong. He likes to throw parties; he invites the local aristocracy. He hosts pheasant shoots. 'Sort of like target practice, really. But it's something to do for a day.' He has the Barbour thornproof jackets, the green Hunter wellington boots.

He bought the house from Lord Hesketh for £15 million. He spent £10 million fixing it up, and another £15 million filling it with objects.

'Poor Hesketh,' says Max, 'gets a really bad rap for losing the house and all that. But it's impossible to maintain a house like this in bits and pieces. You literally have to move everything out, clean it out, spend three years redoing it, and then move back in.'

I tell Max that I like the house. 'It's very manageable to live in, as opposed to Blenheim or Castle Howard,' he says.

I ogle the sculpted hedges and statues, the fruit trees, the gazebo, the medieval church. Max owns a church. There is no congregation. But the bell still works. We walk around. Max picks a peach from a peach tree and gives it to me. I eat the peach.

We go into the house. The wall next to the main staircase is a giant frieze with a recessed marble statue. There are a number of recessed marble statues. If anything, there is too much art. Max owns 'about 140' Old Masters – lots of paintings of Dutch and Italian aristocrats from the eighteenth and nineteenth centuries. He bought them in Sotheby's and Christie's auctions, mostly on the phone, mostly while travelling around the world, overseeing his retail empire.

On the first floor there's a gallery. The windows are sixteen feet tall. I look out at the view, which draws the eye beyond the sculpted hedges and secret gardens and statues, beyond the fountain, along the avenue of ancient trees to the vanishing point on the horizon.

Max shows me his workshop, in the Wren wing, and his desk, above which there are pictures of tall, slender models stuck to a pinboard with pins in their foreheads. There are some pictures of Max with one of the models. This is Natasha. Another Russian. They are making a video together for fun. 'It's called potatoes and caviar,' says Max. 'She shows me her world of eating baked potatoes with salt. And I show her my world. And it turns out that I like baked potatoes with salt.'

We eat lunch in the servants' quarters. Appliances by Charvet and Miele. Nicholas Ash, Max's English butler, has picked salad leaves and plums in the kitchen garden. There are cold cuts of organic meat. Max says he's trying to lose a few pounds. He's slim. 'You would not believe this,' he says, 'but it's possible to gain weight grazing on raspberries.'

Soon we are settled into the staged comfort of the drawing room. There's an Aubusson rug, some oriental urns, an exquisite table displaying an exquisite coffee-table book about country houses, one of which is Easton Neston. There are several Old Master paintings, the largest of which is *The Calydonian Boar Hunt*, painted by Peter Paul Rubens in the 1620s.

I ask Max to sum up his life. He instantly says: 'The pursuit of beauty.'

That's what you'd say?

'Yes.'

He tells me about himself: 'I remember pretty much everything I've ever seen, somewhere in the recesses of my brain.'

As a boy, he hated the Soviet Union. Russians were 'very poorly dressed, and very poorly shod'. At school, he learned English. In the summer, as a teenager, he mixed with Scandinavian tourists. He envied their music, their style – particularly their clothes. They had something he didn't have – 'blue jeans', 'rock'n'roll'. Of course it was more than that. The young Swedes and Danes were expressing themselves in the language of money and sex. They probably didn't even know it. Max knew it better than they did.

They gave him their glossy magazines.

He was desperate to defect. There was a scheme to go to Israel if you were Jewish. Max was Jewish, but he didn't want to go to Israel. So he flew to Vienna, where he was supposed to change planes. But he didn't get on the plane to Israel.

He left behind everything he knew. But that's not quite true. He knew the West. He knew how it worked. He understood us better than we understood ourselves.

His mother had given him three pictures, family photographs, with Fabergé frames. If he could sell the frames, he could get to America.

He remembers being 'in a van, with a guy who's driving me somewhere, and we're driving through Vienna, all of the signage is in German, I don't understand a single word, and suddenly I realised: it was sink or swim. And I think this is precisely the moment when I grew up. This was the moment I became a man.'

Max sold the frames. He made $30,000. He flew to New York. He studied at the Fashion Institute of Technology. Got a job with a fashion company called Manouche. Tried to learn everything about the business. Then he went to Los Angeles to work on a fashion startup called Bis.

At Bis, he did well. He aspired to own a share of the company. But his colleagues would only agree to pay him as an employee. So he left and set up Max Studio. He was twenty-four.

'I had a lot of drive. I wanted to be successful.'

He travelled. Went to China 'very early on'. Quickly saw the possibilities. The factories were 'very primitive, but with an amazing amount of skilful handwork. Anything could be done by hand, and very very well. And dirt cheap.'

Soon he was using 'a dozen' factories, not just in China. He lists the locations: 'Taiwan, Korea, Sri Lanka, Portugal, Turkey, and Central America.' All those hands, stitching and creasing and feeding things into machines, and the hands of Peter Paul Rubens, holding his little brush. All the thousands of hands, working to bring this small Russian to this sitting room in this country house in the English shires.

Max's iPhone pings. 'The model has just got on the train,' he says. This is Natasha.

'Excuse me one second.'

He stares at his phone, sending and receiving texts. He does this for three minutes and twenty-two seconds. Finally he talks to his chauffeur, Roy. Then his phone pings again. Then he sends another text.

He explains his business model. His most expensive dresses cost hundreds of dollars or pounds; never thousands. 'Very high quality,' he says. 'But because we produce vast quantities of product in Asia and China, we have terrific leverage in getting even small quantities done.'

I ask him if he's like Ingvar Kamprad, the founder of Ikea, who, it was said, could look at a design on paper and imagine the entire supply chain leading to its manufacture – the lumberjacks in Poland, the trucking of the timber to manufacturing sites, the cost of the fuel, the warehousing, the exchange rates of the various currencies involved. Then his brain would come up with a price for the finished product, and he'd run the numbers in his head, and be able to make a decision immediately.

'I can do the same. Absolutely can do the same. Yes.'

We talk about textiles. There was the time he managed to get hold of a warehouse full of typewriter ribbon. He turned it into ladies' trousers. He sees his business as 'trying to figure out what I could arbitrage, as it were, in various cultures'.

Ultimately, he makes clothes so that a woman can be 'appropriately dressed for the occasion', but at the same time display 'various degrees of sexiness'.

His phone pings. 'The model has arrived,' he says. She's at the station. She is minutes away.

I ask him if he has a girlfriend.

'No – I'm happily single.'

'How does that work out?'

'Well, maybe I'm uh, slightly used goods, and, yes, should someone worthwhile have me, I will give it a look.'

'Where would you meet somebody?'

'I'm surrounded by beautiful women.'

'What about this Russian girl? Is she the right person?'

'Is she the right person? I don't know. Possibly.'

'Is this a romance?'

'It's, uh, it's, uh … I don't know yet.'

'Potentially?'

'Possibly, yes.'

He's planning to take Natasha on a boat trip around the Mediterranean. Then when the weather gets cold in Europe, he'll go back to Los Angeles. He shows me pictures of his house in Hollywood. It's the Castillo del Lago – the house Bugsy Siegel lived in when he was inventing the modern version of Las Vegas. Max bought the Castillo from the person who bought it from Madonna. He paid $7 million. Before that, he'd been trying to design a house he never built – modernist, with glass boxes. He wanted to build a cinema with a floor made out of some kind of gel that you sink into as you watch the movie. In the end he bought Easton Neston and the Castillo, where he sleeps in the tower.

Max opens a fancy box and takes out a cigarette. 'It's impossible,' he suddenly says. 'To smoke. The girl is coming. I can't smoke. I've given up smoking. She doesn't drink, she doesn't smoke. She's a saint.'

Natasha arrives in the drawing room. She looks like the sort of person who looks very good in photographs. She says hello, and goes off to change into one of Max's frocks.

***

Later, as the sun dips towards the horizon, Max, Nicholas and Natasha pose in front of the house for the picture that will sell my article. The photographer wants to wait until the moment the sun goes down, and bathe the house in artificial light. This is how I will remember Max. He is standing in front of the house, wearing a pale linen suit made in either London or Hong Kong; Natasha is behind him in a lacy, skimpy frock that is appropriate but also conveys a high degree of sexiness. Feminine allure. Max has a scientific understanding of the power it has. Not just over men. But over women. Nicholas is holding a tray.

The picture is real but also not real. In a few minutes, Natasha will ask Roy to take her back to the station. After that, Nicholas will make dinner for himself and Max. Nicholas will eat in the servants' quarters; Max will dine alone in the dining room.

I look at Max. The man who created a supply chain. Every supply chain makes one person richer than everybody else in the chain. And for an infinitely brief moment, everything – Max, Nicholas, Natasha, the frock, the house – are bathed in artificial light.

'That's perfect,' says the photographer.

***

Celia calls one afternoon while I'm walking through the grounds of
a ruined castle. That sounds odd, I know, but it's not – I live near
a ruined castle, so I'm always cutting through its grounds. Most of
the time I don't even think about it.

But when my phone rings, I stop, and look around, and I see
that's where I am, inside the broken walls, the old tower looming
behind me.

'William?'

'Yes?'

She must be calling because she has a particular question to ask
me, or perhaps an offer to make. The plausible spectrum, from
negative to positive, is huge. Someone might be suing me. Someone
from the government or the tax authorities might be stalking me
via my contacts. This has happened before. On the other hand,
she's much more likely to be offering me a story – or even money
itself. Sometimes I'm owed an amount of money that has somehow
got diverted, and is now on its way. This might be the reason for
the call.

I press the phone into my ear.

'Yes?'

'William – would you say you were an anxious person?'

'What?'

'Do you suffer from anxiety?'

Technically, I know the answer to this question. The answer is
'yes'. And for some reason, right now I'm going through an anxiety
spike. This was true even before I felt my phone buzzing in my
pocket. If Celia could have seen me this morning! Checking the
dials and switches in my kitchen. I still wanted to check them after
I'd left the house.

I know the protocol – don't give in to the dials and switches.
They want to take up space in your head. Don't let them. Don't let
them control you. They are designed so that *you* can control *them*.

A social scientist, on the other hand, might say, OK – but there
are an awful lot of these dials and switches, aren't there? The cooker,
the oven, the washing machine, the tumble dryer, plus the different
remotes. All the volume controls and dimmer switches. The

gaming 'controllers', which want to butt in and replace some of the duties of the incumbent remote control devices, and the control panels that creep into your phone without being asked – they're all clamouring for attention and status, like a pack of baboons. That's what a zoologist might well call them, all the controls and controllers. A pack of baboons.

I must have owned twenty remotes, and I don't know the whereabouts of at least eighteen of them. Two or three might be in boxes in my garage – if that. The rest of them could be anywhere. Some must be in landfill sites, great underground cities of trash – I suppose the displaced soil must be taken somewhere else and used for other purposes. Landscaping, is my guess. Anyway, that probably accounts for five remotes. So where are the other eleven? A few must have broken into pieces and made their way into the sea via rivers and sewers. A lot of plastic makes its way to the sea – there's a vast roiling mass of it, a plastic island the size of Texas. It's the opposite of Treasure Island. As it gets bigger, the size of the bits of plastic gets smaller, because of the actual roiling, until the bits are small enough to get into the food chain – the fish eat the tiny bits of plastic, and we eat the fish, and bits of old TV remotes pass through our alimentary canal, and make their way into the sewers, travelling back to the roiling plastic Texas, like eels returning to the Sargasso Sea.

Again, I'm not a social scientist, but I'm pretty sure this sequence is lodged in the backs of all our minds, we all know it's happening, we all know it's getting worse, and this must contribute to the general level of anxiety in the developed world. We're creating this roiling island, which is killing the planet, and we know it, and we're also denying it, and the bigger the island gets, the more denial we need to employ, and this denial is not without cost. Like when you run over an animal, and you could stop, and turn around, and check it out, or you could just drive on – in which case you need to block out the imagined pain of the animal for the time it would take the animal to die. But the thing about the planet is that it never stops dying. On one level, we can always hear its screams.

I'm not an economist, but I know the reason for the roiling island. It's the fact that the economy needs to grow, because almost every company that makes things is in debt, and must make more things in order to pay off the snowballing interest – and typically they make things from plastic, and they hire advertising executives to think of clever ways to sell the bits of plastic, and models to wear or pose with the bits of plastic, and photographers to take pictures of the models, the bits of plastic having been turned by designers into tights and frocks, or handheld controllers, and they will all be eaten by fish, and then by us, and then flushed away, increasing the size of the roiling island and adding to the general level of anxiety in the world.

Not long ago, I was asked to do a story on a guy called David de Rothschild, a member of the richest family in the world, because he, de Rothschild, wanted to do something about the roiling island. He'd come up with a brilliant idea. He was building a catamaran, a sort of cool dude's boat, out of plastic bottles, which made me think of Mr Gilmour, the Canadian billionaire who let me stay on his private island and visit his bottling factory in Fiji. I thought of all the bottling factories, the way they move the clear plastic blanks towards the section that turns them into hollow shapes, and then towards the pressurised water jet, on the way to the lid machine. And de Rothschild was constructing a catamaran out of plastic bottles, and was then going to sail this catamaran through the Pacific Ocean, navigating his way towards the roiling island.

He was very good-looking, David de Rothschild, by the way. So this was the plot of *Treasure Island* in reverse. This was not ugly pirates with missing limbs seeking buried treasure, but an extremely handsome man, already enormously rich, sailing the seven seas towards an island of no value whatsoever, in fact an island of anti-value, made from things that had been flushed away.

De Rothschild was hoping to draw the world's attention to the island of anti-value. A brilliant idea. A guy I know asked me if de Rothschild was very tall. Yes, I said – he is very tall. The guy I know had been to a Rothschild wedding, he said, in Switzerland, maybe

Gstaad or somewhere, and he said they were all tall, the Rothschilds. They'd started out short, he said, in the eighteenth century, but the men always married tall glamorous models, because rich men always attract tall glamorous models, and now the whole family was tall and glamorous.

Anyway, de Rothschild built his cool dude's boat out of plastic bottles. Then he sailed to the island of anti-value to raise awareness. Journalists wrote about him – and about the island. But the island is still there. It does not attract many visitors. There is no buried treasure on the island. In the meantime, it is still in the back of our collective mind, getting bigger, and the general level of our anxiety is rising.

Holding the phone to my ear, I cast my eyes around the grounds of the ruined castle. There must have been a point when the people in the castle were anxious – particularly when somebody invented the cannon. Before the cannon, as long as you were inside the castle, you were fine. But then, suddenly, you were just as safe outside the castle – probably even safer. People must have sat around campfires reminiscing about the days when you were safe in the castle, as long as nobody shot an arrow directly through one of the slits in the tower. And even then you'd have to be passing the slit at that precise moment. Other than that, you were safe.

Centuries ago, you usually knew where the boundaries were, where the enemy could get you. Now, of course, the enemy is everywhere – the enemy can get into your phone without you knowing.

He can get into your *head* without you knowing.

So, yes, I'm anxious in the way that most of us are anxious. But I'm also anxious beyond that point.

I'm anxious to the point of self-sabotage. I have a mechanism in my head that wants me to be poor. The mechanism would like me to be a derelict – homeless, living under a bridge. That's how anxious I am.

Something is wrong, and I don't know how it works.

These thoughts flicker through my mind at warp speed.

I don't know how it works, and I don't *want* to know how it works. In any case, I tell myself, we're all anxious. Anxiety is the core of the human condition, because we know we're going to die. And modern death is worse than ancient death, because now it takes so long. It takes years. Most people are dying for at least a quarter of their lives. Better the arrow through the slit in the tower. Ten minutes of pectoral agony and that's it.

The modern condition consists of creeping slowly towards death, haunted by death and the roiling island, in denial about the control panels and the discarded devices.

I met this guy, Joel, who was fascinated by discarded devices. He had a brilliant idea for what to do with them. He particularly liked TV sets, out-of-date computers, things with screens and old music systems. He would hire a van and drive around London. People just leave these things in the street. I spent a few hours with him, picking things up. He also liked washing machines, dishwashers, fridges, tumble dryers and microwave ovens. Unwanted cubes with dials and switches.

We drove around and picked up these unwanted cubes and screens and put them in the van. The cubes and screens were everywhere. As a society, the problem we have is getting rid of them.

Joel took all the cubes and screens to a warehouse he'd hired. He filled it with unwanted technology. In the Third World, people would still be using this stuff. In Japan, they might have got rid of it earlier. It depends on the quality of the advertising in a given place, the ability of advertisers to get you to stop liking the cubes and screens you've already got.

Joel called his idea Scrap Club. He roped off an area in the middle of the warehouse, and filled it with cubes and screens. A sort of boxing ring. He invited people to enter the ring and destroy the cubes. He gave them a huge mallet and protective clothing.

People queued up and paid him. You got three minutes. There was an audience. When it was someone's turn, the person would step into the ring and smash all these cubes and screens with the mallet. Heavy metal music would be blasting. Afterwards people would get all the smashed stuff out of the ring and put more TV sets and computers and microwaves in there.

A compressed memory flashes through my mind. It's my turn. Wearing my protective suit and mask, I step into the ring, holding the mallet. The music blasts and scrapes. I lift the mallet. I swing. I smash a TV set right in the screen, a nice sideways swipe, and then I take out a couple of monitors, raising the mallet and smashing down, raising and smashing, it's a blur, I'm attacking the cubes and screens, distorting and crushing them, hurting them, exposing their guts, the white and coloured wires, the mallet perfect in my hands, beating down on the metal and glass, tormenting the metal and glass, atomising the dials and switches, people are watching me and I do not want this to end, I can feel a great rush of something good, have not felt better, more whole, in a long time, and when I step out of the ring I'm trembling.

Now I look out beyond the ruined castle to the blue hills. Something is wrong. I need to know how it works.

'Yes,' I say to Celia. 'Yes. I would say that I'm anxious.'

***

On the way to the country-house anxiety retreat Celia has arranged for me, I try to make mental notes about my anxiety.

I'm frightened of something.

I don't know what it is.

Of course, what you *think* you're frightened of is never what you're really frightened of.

There's always something underneath, something you can't think about. But you must think about it. But you can't. But you must. That's psychoanalysis. You must think about the thing you can't think about. You must look at the thing your mind doesn't want you to see.

That's what I believe. And that's what I dread. I believe and dread that, in order to fix yourself, you must go back into the past, travel the routes of disorder and dysfunction and find the thing your mind wants to protect you from. Locate the mechanism that drives you.

The mechanism that *is* you.

I take a taxi, and a train, and another train, and another taxi, and then I'm in the countryside moving towards a range of blue hills in the distance.

The things I tell myself I fear: death and disease. Heights. Enclosed spaces. Being trapped in a tunnel or a mine.

Also, I am haunted by the idea of waking up in a coffin. Something about the fact that you are lying on your back. You can't even turn around; you are denied even that crumb of comfort. In 'The Premature Burial', Edgar Allan Poe describes a coffin that has, for some reason, been unearthed. There are scratch marks on the lid. It turns out, the narrator says, that lots of coffins have scratch marks on the lid. Now ask yourself the killer question: what percentage of coffins are dug up? Maybe 1 per cent. At most.

Which means that, at any one time, hundreds or even thousands of people are trapped, in coffins, six feet underground, for days and days, until they die. And nobody will ever know. Nobody will ever see those scratch marks.

When I was a kid, I was distracted by a fear of blindness. This fear became a driving obsession. I kept imagining what everything would look like in your mind's eye when your actual eyes had stopped working. The images would distort and corrupt. They would be subject to glitches of memory. Someone would take you to a favourite beauty spot, a country house or a beach, and you would have nothing but your memory of the house or the beach, which would have rotted away in your mind's eye, probably affected by your depression at being blind. The house would look dark and haunted, or streaked with demonic colours; the stonework would be uneven and crumbling at the edges. The beach would not be a beautiful arc of sand lapped by crystal blue; it would be a beach in a nightmare. It would be pulverised shells bordering dark water full of small creatures being chased by bigger creatures, which in turn would be being chased and caught and torn apart by even bigger creatures. So the world would no longer be the world as it appeared to you; it would be a scale model, a diorama improvised from the diminishing store of elements you could glean from your own haunted mind. This anxiety fixated me between the ages of eleven and sixteen; it went away until the age of twenty, when it was triggered again by Henry Green's novel *Blindness*. When I read *Blindness*, my fear of blindness, partly real and partly nostalgic, flared up again for a couple of months. Anyway, by the age of twenty I had become obsessed with other diseases and conditions.

There was always a leading disease, and the only way I could stop myself being frightened of this disease was to replace it with another disease I feared even more. I developed a method – I would read medical textbooks, looking for a disease worse than the one that currently preoccupied me. There would be a moment of relief, when my brain was confused between the two diseases. But the relief would not last long – and, of course, my new fear would turn out to be more extreme than my last.

Added to this, I had a strong sense that people were observing and pursuing me – in reality, and also in my dreams. I would often wake from a dream in which I was about to be executed. For years, the executions were formal and respectful. There would be a knock on my cell door; I would be led towards a scaffold. Then my head would be placed in a noose. More recently, the executions have been much rougher. They happen suddenly, in car parks and shopping malls. Men with guns snatch me, drag me into dark corners.

A small sample of my fears. The tip of the iceberg – which is itself an elaborate pretence, protecting me from whatever is underneath the iceberg, whatever it is that my brain doesn't want me to see.

My taxi slows down and turns into an avenue of trees. We are approaching the retreat – an old country house, a classic design, from the 18th century.

We drive down the avenue. I get out of the taxi with my wheeled luggage. I'm standing in front of a lovely house with two wings, a courtyard in the middle. In front of the house is a drive, with a line of new black German cars – a Porsche, a Mercedes, two Audis, a BMW. I walk up the path to the house, my wheeled luggage rattling behind.

Something clicks in my mind, and for a moment, arriving at this strange institution, an exact emotion is unearthed, the feeling of arrival at my first boarding school at the age of ten. My family were hundreds of miles away, in a different country; for a time I would have to forget about their existence. Perhaps I actually needed to forget about their existence. I had travelled with my mother's cousin; she was the one who dropped me at the school, adding to the general sense of confusion. Then she was gone. I was relieved; I could tell how sad she was.

I felt like a person who was not exactly the person he had been, or thought he was. I would sleep in a dormitory for twelve weeks, at the end of which I would be able to go home. But that's the thing people mostly don't understand. You never really go home. Home is not the same place as it was before.

As I enter the retreat, a familiar sense of bleakness, of having nothing to hope for, flashes through my mind and lodges somewhere in my gut.

Nothing to hope for. Nothing to trust. What a fool you were to trust things in the past. Not a mistake you will make again. These are your feelings, and these are the feelings you hate yourself for having.

If anybody knew you had these feelings, if anybody ever found out …

Jesus, these are ugly thoughts. I open the door and enter the open space beyond. It's lovely, in its chintzy way. Not the same as Max's house, which hits you with a fusillade of money. This space is more comforting. I check in and walk up the curved staircase to my room – big bed, sofa, chairs, desk, bathroom. There are views across the formal gardens, with blue hills in the distance.

Later, there's an informal get-together of anxious people – and some of those who will be advising and treating us – in a downstairs drawing room. We mill around, shake hands, drink cups of tea in delicate china teacups. I am enveloped by a new layer of anxiety – the anxiety that comes with being a reporter, as well as a client. These people will be opening up, in front of me, revealing the depths of their torment. I have said that I will not identify them personally. But how much comfort would this be, really? I am, I might say to them, very good at moving from the particular to the general; I can use specific details, while at the same time not going too far. Still, in the past I have often made mistakes. Sometimes, caught up in the moment, I have gone too far. But I will *try* not to.

The anxious people are mostly rich or very rich. Three or four are traders of money in the banking system; something about swapping one type of money for another has made their brains crack under the strain. One is the spouse of a money trader whose brain has not cracked; whose brain, in fact, is a beautifully efficient machine for trading money. But the spouse has cracked. One or two people are part of a supply chain that has recently been re-jigged, meaning that they no longer control the supply chain. Someone who has better access to data, or more powerful computers, is putting the squeeze on them. And now they have to fire people, or make these people work harder, which is horrible. They hate it. And the squeeze is getting tighter. And they are cracking under the strain.

And then there's me. I've been anxious for decades; I function very well, and sometimes very badly. I am super-competent. But there are cracks. I let things go. Bad things happen. Mostly, I am emotionally distant; people sometimes see me as cold. I have become one of life's observers. I look at people and try to imagine what it's like to be them. I have a strong sense that, if ever I'm successful, I will pay for it – somewhere, deep down, I am driven by guilt. Some deep part of my mind, I suppose my unconscious, is perpetually trying to balance the books by flooding my thoughts with obsessions and compulsions, most of which I have learned to ignore. It's a grim, chronic war – which I think I'm winning. But every so often I lose a battle. Sometimes I lose two or three in a row. Meanwhile, my finances suffer. Money seeps away. I regroup. I press on.

Back in my room, after dinner, I look out of my window. Trees and clipped hedges made eerie by moonlight. I lie on my bed. As always, I'm thankful not to be sleeping in a dormitory. Another wave of dark nostalgia passes through me – the bitter tincture of loneliness, mixed with the usual guilt, and an obscure envy of my younger self, who had so much to come. A song from my first week in the dormitory embeds itself in my brain: 'Knock Three Times'. Then another: 'Hot Love'. Some boys had tiny radios which they hid during the day, then listened to at night. Nobody understood about sex. But they talked about it incessantly. The older matron was anti-masturbation, and made the boy in the bed opposite me write 'I must not play with my parts' fifty times in neat handwriting. The assistant matron, a French girl, bathed us with enthusiasm and tenderness, half-pretending, I think, not to notice my erection – or my mounting excitement at the soapy hand that brushed against it.

I'm beginning to be uncomfortable, lying on the bed in my clothes. But I don't want to go through the rigmarole of getting up and cleaning my teeth.

Those schools, I see now, were designed to perform a specific function. They performed it very well. They churned out thousands of emotionally cold young men who would go on to run the engine of empire, setting up those supply chains across the globe and organising those supply chains to maximum advantage, sucking every last drop of wealth from the poorest countries. They built and administered railways to move wealth out of India, they built telegraph networks to move data faster than Africans who used drums or semaphore. The schools taught you to withstand hardship and also to memorise and organise endless details. By the age of twelve, you knew your Latin and French grammar, you could recite poetry by heart, you knew about the Roman empire, the Tudors and Stuarts, Napoleon and Nelson. They were good at what they did, those schools. You have to give them that.

When I was ten, I was not sexually abused by a predatory teacher. Others were. Eventually one boy was abducted and the predator was sent to jail. We were too young to fully understand his drives, although we had some hazy, unspoken idea. The way he checked to see that boys were not wearing underpants in PE lessons. The way he grabbed and squeezed certain boys. One evening, during prep, the predatory guy was invigilating. He loomed up behind me. I could see his arms coming towards me. His body language. He could only want to hug me from behind. And I was filled with fury. As his arms closed around me, I jabbed at him. Hard in the stomach. Not just once. I grunted at him to get away from me.

People looked up to see what had happened, and then down again, and the guy walked away.

The moment passed.

But I hadn't expected to feel so angry, or so righteous. And it wasn't for years, decades, that I understood what it was I was actually angry about.

In the morning, we sit at tables in a drawing room in one of Thomas White's wings. A psychologist called Amanda Collins tells us about anxiety. We will have daily classes with Collins, as well as one-on-one sessions with Charles Linden, who has set up the retreat. Collins and Linden both suffered from anxiety. Collins could not stop blushing; knowing she was going to blush made her blush even more. Linden was anxious as a child, and had a breakdown in his early twenties. For a time, he stayed in his bedroom, too frightened even to go to the bathroom, even to empty his bladder. His girlfriend, Beth, would visit him in her lunch break and supervise a bathroom visit.

Now Linden has devised a method for getting rid of anxiety. If you practise the Linden Method, he says, your chances of overcoming anxiety, of banishing it totally, are 100 per cent.

As Collins talks, I take notes and doodle on my pad. I draw a circle and imagine it's a brain. The thing about the brain is that it's made up of tens of billions of neurons. A thought happens when a set of neurons are connected together. So if, say, I have a thought about my ten-year-old self in the dormitory, this thought happens because, in a millisecond, hundreds of thousands of neurons are connected together. Each neuron contributes to the thought, and no two thoughts connect exactly the same set of neurons, so no two thoughts can be exactly alike. But still, the more often you have a certain type of thought, the stronger the connection between certain neurons becomes. So if you tend to have anxious thoughts over and over, you're more likely to have anxious thoughts in the future.

The way you think is a set of habits.

I'm pondering this when Amanda Collins tells us what I will come to believe is the mainstay of the Linden Method.

She says: do not try to get to the bottom of your anxious thoughts. Do not spend any more time searching for the origins of your anxiety. Forget it. It's pointless.

Why do it? What do you think will happen when you finally come to the end of your search? If you ever do, that is.

The answer, according to the Linden Method, is: nothing.

So: stop thinking about what it is that's making you anxious. Think about something else instead. And then: keep thinking about something else. Try different things. Experiment. Do what works for you. Keep on doing what works for you.

When Amanda Collins says this, a light goes on and off in my head.

Over the next three days, Collins and Linden tell us how to practise the Linden Method. It becomes clear. It's not about fixing the dysfunctional mechanism in your head. It's about ignoring it.

If you ignore the mechanism, it will wither and die. You don't need to kill it. You just need to starve it of attention.

Put all of your mental energy into thinking about something else – about the things that work, rather than the things that don't work. Of course, you have to find something that works – something that will compete with the dysfunctional thoughts you had before. This will take practice. You will need to practise thinking new thoughts, over and over again, trying this and that, looking for something that works. That, as far as I can see, is the Linden Method.

In the spa, I lie on my front while a young woman massages me. She oils her hands and works on my neck and back while I think about mastering the Linden Method. I need to have a revolution in my head. I need to look forward, rather than back.

Don't be like those medieval monks, looking through the old books over and over, by candlelight, in their damp, old rooms. Forget the past. It's ancient history. It doesn't exist any more.

But, I'm thinking.

But I don't *feel* like somebody who can just get up and walk away from the past. The past has its claws in me.

The past *is* me.

The past is what I feel. The past is my emotions. Remorse and fear. Remorse at my actions, fear of the consequences of my actions. And, of course, my inactions. Remorse and fear because of what I did and did not do. Remorse and fear weighing me down. Remorse and fear in the morning. Remorse and fear during the day. Remorse and fear late at night.

Remorse plus fear equals guilt.

To look into my mind right now is to look into a deep crevasse of guilt. Guilt at infiltrating a group of anxious people in order to write about them; guilt that I'm pretending to be someone I'm not, or not quite; guilt that I'm hurting these people, that I'm selling them out, guilt that they are telling me their secrets, and I'm taking mental notes so I can sell these secrets. Underlying this layer of guilt is the guilt that I'm hoping to use these secrets to attract the attention of my reader to these people, these poor anxious people, in order to divert my reader's attention to the glossy ads that have been carefully crafted to make him or her feel inadequate; guilt therefore that I'm not selling my work, but selling my reader; that I am, at this moment, conning a group of vulnerable people, people whose anxiety is so acute they have paid thousands of pounds to stay at an anxiety retreat, trying to get away from a world that threatens them, I'm conning them and then heartlessly using them to attract the attention of my readers to forces that are designed to beguile them, to make *them* feel anxious and vulnerable, which will make them spend money in order to fend off this growing anxiety and vulnerability, if only for a little while.

Here I am, in a spa, being palpated by oiled fingers, the oiled fingers of a young woman; here I am, the sellout, the turncoat, the quisling, sitting on my ledge of guilt, peering into the crevasse below, and I hate the idea but I must lower myself down, a bad person sliding down in the dark, and I don't know what's down there, but of course I do, it's the thing, the mechanism, the creature that lives in me, that controls me, the bully who intimidates my inner coward, who tells me to stay in bed, who tells me to bring my books into my bed and stay there, curtains drawn, who switches my alarm clock off, who pulls me away from my desk when I try to write, who is always offering me a drink, hey, what about a tincture, a stiffener, or what about something better, there's always something better, and here I am, sliding down in the dark, sliding down, all present and correct, ready to fail, to flunk, to take the easy option, and one day soon it will be too late, I'm hanging by a thread, maybe it's already too late, the thread will snap, has it snapped? I will become, maybe already have become, one of those guys, the guy who had it but threw it away, the life and soul of the smelly old bar.

This is what I'm thinking as the oiled hands slide up and down my back and neck. The deep crevasse I'm thinking. The murk at the bottom of the crevasse I'm thinking.

The creature that lives in the murk. I feel the fingers on my back, sliding upwards, pressing into my neck, and I breathe, slowly and deeply, and look into the murk, and there it is, a face in the shadows, in the dark mirror, I can see it, I must turn, turn and walk away, never look back, never look at it again. It's me.

***

For several days, I practise the Linden Method. There are 'Ten Pillars'. Stop seeing therapists. Stop taking medications. Stop researching anxiety. Only follow the Linden Method. Stop talking about your anxiety. Don't lean on other people. Don't hold on to your memories. Divert your mind. Develop new habits.

My pillars: starve the mechanism, the evil creature inside you, of attention. Kill the old superstitions. Look out at the world. Collect data. Exploit the data. Move forward.

You are a shark.

I sit down in the drawing room and talk to Charles Linden. He is a tall, good-looking alpha male with a shaved head. He tells me about his own childhood. 'I started making inappropriate risk assessments,' he says. For instance, he developed a fear of rope swings. This was the start.

'I was seeing the world through anxiety-coloured specs,' he says. Later, he developed school phobia. He told his mum he wanted to die. Things got worse. At the age of thirteen, Linden worried he might be poisoned in the chemistry lab, or electrocuted. He thought he might be killed on the rugby field. He checked his school lunch for poison. Every day he went to the school nurse and called his mother, asking to be taken home. He never was.

Linden tells me he was always looking for, and always failing to find, 'a safe place to go'.

Anxiety, he says, is a condition in which the sufferer is always looking for that safe place to go. When Linden left home, he went to Heidelberg, where he studied German. But his anxiety deepened. One day, at a petrol station, he collapsed with a panic attack. Back home in England, things got better, and then worse. Eventually he discovered neuroplasticity. The brain changes when you change your thoughts.

He changed his thoughts. He didn't stop. He moved forward relentlessly, like a shark.

You need to stop looking for safety and reassurance, he says – the safe haven the anxious brain yearns for.

'There isn't one,' he says. 'When you're born, the umbilical cord is cut, and you're on your own.'

I shake hands with the anxious people for the final time. The money traders and company directors, and the spouse of the money trader who is not anxious at all, who has everything under control. They have all spent £2,800 on the anxiety retreat. So £30,000, give or take, for Charles Linden.

The German cars draw away from the retreat. My taxi picks me up.

Something is wrong, I think as I drive down the avenue of trees.

Something is wrong. The mechanism. The evil creature. I could spend my life trying to find out how it works.

Or I could do something else. I could starve it of attention. That's what I'm thinking as I look back, trying to get a final glimpse of the retreat.

Starve it of attention.

Then move on.

5

I'm sitting on a terrace, on a beach, on a tiny private island, fifty miles north of the equator. It's the dry season, so the air feels clean, and the pressure is high, which is good, because even though it's hot today, the air feels just crisp enough that it's not *overly* hot.

Also there's a slight breeze, again not too much but just right, a whisper of air in my ear, telling me not to worry, everything's fine, and the sea is whispering too, repeating its mantra, shh-shush, shh-shush, and the sea is saying the exact same thing as the air, the sea is saying don't worry, it's fine; don't worry, it's fine.

My feet are in a plunge pool. In theory, I don't agree with plunge pools – why not just plunge into the sea? After all, it's yards away, it might as well be at the bottom of the garden. But in practice, I actually like plunge pools.

Why?

Sometimes you want to get wet in a controlled way, or on a sudden whim, or while you're still in the shade. And remember, it's good to sit on the edge of the plunge pool and put your feet in the water while you're reading a book.

The downside is that, if you ran a statistical analysis, you'd find that the plunge pool makes you go into the sea a bit less than you would without it. You get out of bed, and immerse yourself in the plunge pool, and then get out of the plunge pool, put on a bathrobe, and make yourself a cup of coffee. Ideally, you'd jump into the sea after you got out of bed and before you made the coffee.

But you don't.

So you miss out on one of the best things life has to offer – getting into the sea – and replace it, at least sometimes, with something sub-optimal: the plunge pool.

Consider this: if you had a good restaurant right next door to your house, you would spend less time in the great restaurant down the road. With the best will in the world, you just would.

I move my feet in the water and put my book down, splayed open, on the edge of the plunge pool. The author is a fascinating guy. I met him recently, although right now I want to put *that* incident out of my mind.

I look at the sky and the beach and the sea in front of me, and I turn and look behind at the little house I'm staying in – my personal 'beach studio'. It really is excellent, my beach studio, although whenever I walk around it, my mind is divided in two, part of me being in the here and now, and part of me thinking what other people would think if they could see it, could see me in it. I take photographs of it, but I don't send them to people. I'm not that sort of person. I take photographs and *imagine* sending them to people, is what I do.

I have a large double bed, I think king size but I'm not sure, and I have a TV I never watch but that looks lovely, a cold fridge full of treats, a perfect Wi-Fi connection, a glass-topped desk, beautiful varnished wooden flooring. At the back of the beach studio is a walled garden in the Japanese style, which is actually a bathroom, there are two sinks and two mirrors and a bathtub and an outdoor shower, and nobody can see you, you can walk around this Japanese garden, have a shower, have a bath, clean your teeth, take photographs of yourself in the mirror – feel free!

Every so often I walk into the Japanese garden and think about my bathroom at home. I must update my bathroom at home – another thing on my to-do list. Write a bestseller. Update my bathroom. Make millions – I can do it! Cut the carbs. Abolish belly fat. Go Paleo. Eat raw – there's a good reason why this works. Get back in touch with the author of the book I'm reading. Get inside his head. Pick his brain.

The author is Nassim Nicholas Taleb. The book is *The Black Swan*. It's one of my favourite books. I'm reading it for the third time, and I am, I think, only just beginning to understand it.

It's about human beings, who don't know how the world works. They really don't. And that's a problem.

But there's a deeper problem. The deeper problem is not that we don't know how the world works. The deeper problem is that we think we do.

We look at the world. We believe we see regularities. We formulate rules. But the rules we formulate don't describe reality. We've made them up in our minds. We are like Bertrand Russell's chicken. Except Taleb updates Russell's chicken. He imagines a Thanksgiving turkey. The farmer feeds the turkey for a thousand days. The turkey looks for patterns and formulates rules. The rules tell him that the farmer loves him. The rules tell him that the farmer has his best interests at heart.

Every day, his belief in the rules is stronger than it was the day before.

The turkey is like a scientist who conducts a thousand experiments. He creates a model of the world.

And the model works perfectly.

Until it doesn't.

I move my feet in the plunge pool. The water flows around my ankles. The sea sounds like it's saying shh-shush, shh-shush. The sea sounds like it's saying don't worry, it's fine, everything is OK.

If you were the turkey, what happens on the thousand-and-first day would come out of the blue. It would feel like an outlier – even though it is the whole point, the central meaning, of your life. That, says Taleb, is the pattern of human history. It is dominated by outliers we didn't see coming.

Taleb calls these outliers Black Swans. (In medieval England, the expression 'about as likely as a black swan' was a bit like saying 'when pigs fly'. People had no idea that, on the other side of the world, swans actually *were* black.)

Think of anything important, says Taleb – in history, or in your own life. Did you expect it? Did it arrive on schedule? No – it came out of the blue, didn't it?

A Black Swan has three characteristics. It comes out of the blue, it has a massive impact, and then, afterwards, we try to tell ourselves that we should have been able to predict it.

Our lives are dominated by Black Swans. But our minds can't face this information; our actual brains aren't built to handle it. So we keep telling ourselves life takes place within the bounds of the normal.

We focus on the normal, and deny the outlier, even though the outlier is more important.

The outlier is the main event. But we can't see it coming. So we pretend it's not there.

But it's always there, just around the corner.

I'm on this island, in the Maldives, in the Indian Ocean, to write about the island and create envy in the reader of the *Financial Times*, who might read my article and decide to come to the Maldives for a short break. It would have to be a short break – this place is tiny. I remember I once spent a week on a tropical island with a girlfriend, and on the fourth day, I think it was the fourth day, we realised that something had gone wrong with the travel arrangements, some booking I'd forgotten to make, and after a morning on the phone I had to break the bad news; we wouldn't be able to leave the island for a further week. And now the island began to feel like a prison. The crescent of sand, the crystal blue sea – how horrid they looked. Those local dishes – how could we have thought them charming? Or eaten them at all? On the fourth and fifth days, we sat in our room, drinking and smoking and snapping at each other. I arranged for a rich friend to wire me money so I could book a flight. If I spent enough money, we could escape from the island. I spent the money that was not mine. It was thousands. But we could escape.

And now the beach started to look good again. The crescent of sand, the crystal blue. How lovely it all was. The hermit crabs! The palm trees! By the sixth day, it had regained the perfection we had granted it on day one. Now we didn't want to leave. That's how it felt. Of course, we did want to leave. But we didn't want to leave. That's how it felt.

This island is tiny. You can swim, read, watch television, go on the Internet. You can have an outdoor shower. You can walk naked around your Japanese garden – not a good experience if you're even slightly overweight. You keep catching glimpses of yourself in one of the mirrors. I'm slightly overweight. Slim, I'd enjoy this place twice as much.

There's a library, a spa, several restaurants. One restaurant is a sort of hunter-gatherer barbecue pit. There's a place where you can play giant-size video games – like, you can take a penalty against a full-scale virtual goalkeeper. I have already learned to outfox this robot opponent.

There's an underwater nightclub. To get to this place, you need to take a motor boat out into the sea. Of course, you can't see the nightclub from the beach. But there's some sort of platform, and then I guess you walk down a staircase. I've arranged to meet someone at the hunter-gatherer meat place, a representative of the resort, and he will tell me all about the underwater nightclub, and the next day, or the one after that, I'll get on the boat and head towards the platform.

The hunter-gatherer place is half-indoors and half-outdoors. There are thick chunks of meat. Actual hunter-gatherers on this island would have fished; they'd have been fisher-gatherers. This meat must be shipped in from hundreds of miles away; there are no cows or herds of buffalo here. But still. It makes you think of tribal people, of one's primal self, of the guy in the tribe who was the best hunter, who'd have given thick chunks of meat to people he favoured – like the person who was good at building shacks. Some people would hunt; others would gather. Women? Maybe. Matt Ridley believes the division of labour between early human males and females fomented a deep understanding of trade and was the key to our success as a species. Also that this was, very likely, exactly what the Neanderthals didn't have. They were just as clever as us, they made clothes, they were artistic, but they didn't have this division of labour, so they didn't understand trade, didn't specialise, didn't progress. Ultimately they sat in caves, beetle-browed, paintbrush in hand, Van Gogh-like, starving to death. But look at the descendants of *homo erectus*. Here we are, on an island, in a hunter-gatherer barbecue pit, with a pixelated goalkeeper and an underwater nightclub, eating thick chunks of meat.

Here's the representative of the resort. I ask him how one goes about creating an underwater nightclub. First, he says, you build it. Then you put it underwater.

I eat my meat.

The next day I walk around my Japanese garden. I take a shower. I sit with my feet in the plunge pool, reading and doodling.

Black Swans, says Taleb, are the key to understanding the human condition. Which, incidentally, must mean they are the key to getting rich.

I think of the people I have interviewed who got rich: Gilmour, Dennis, Sugar, Schultz, Belfort, Max. They all focused on something until they could see it very clearly, they spotted something others had not noticed, and then they did something novel and unexpected, they *acted* – and rode along on a cascade of events, all of which worked in their favour.

The Bruce Lee poster folded to look like a magazine. The hi-fi decks made by the people who normally make butter dishes. Pitching five-dollar stocks to rich people. Marketing water as a luxury item. Encouraging people to spend a lot more time, and therefore a lot more money, in coffee shops.

Innovations that came out of the blue, that changed whole market sectors. But people in those sectors will tell themselves, every time, that they should have seen it coming.

I look out at the sea.

I'm thinking that if you take any corner of the world, and look at it long enough, with the right kind of intensity, pretty soon you'll see something nobody else has noticed.

In the evening, I get on the boat that takes you to the underwater nightclub. There are a handful of people on the boat. We make progress across the dark water, under the dark sky. In real life, one must travel to a nightclub. On holiday, they are just there. Here, one must travel. Ergo, this feels more like real life. And, at the same time, less like real life. I have mixed feelings about nightclubs anyway. Are they really just about sex? The music is a menu, telling you about the sex you might or might not have later on, might or might not enjoy, might or might not regret, and, thinking this, a song flashes into my mind, I can see the video, long legs and high heels, pretty faces looking in the mirror.

I alight on the platform. Something makes me think of oil rigs. There is, of course, no queue of mini-skirted women trying to catch the eye of the bouncer, no bouncer, no shifty coke dealers, no taxis double-parked outside, no velvet rope to be ceremoniously unclipped, allowing the sexual superstar that is you to descend regally into the inferno.

I walk down the stairs.

At the bottom of the stairs is a bar with tables and chairs, and ladies' and gents' restrooms, and big windows, so you can see the fish swimming around outside. The water is lit up, as in an aquarium. The atmosphere is of a hotel lobby, with a good view of the fish outside. The modern world, it strikes me not for the first time, aspires to be like a hotel lobby. You could bring your laptop in here and work. I might actually do that. Work down here. The place might stir my creative juices. In fact, it already has: I just thought of a business idea, which might be good, or perhaps the worst idea in the world. Elements of Jacques Cousteau and Howard Schultz. I will mull it over.

I look around at the other people. They are underwater. They are rich. They like being dry.

I wonder how the staff deal with the sewage from the restrooms. Does it just go into the sea? Or do they bring it up during the day, and put it on the boat? And then what? Take it where?

***

The next day I upgrade to a more luxurious island. I get on a fast white boat. We cut through water the colour of sapphires. There are lots of islands, hundreds of them, thousands, and even more not-quite-islands, sandbars so close to being underwater they don't count as islands. Everybody here knows that, if the water rose just a few inches, lots of the actual islands would disappear. When the water rises, this will be the first place to disappear. This is the outpost.

I think: every puff of exhaust coming out of this boat might be the one that tips the balance.

What's my excuse? Living as a member of the 1 per cent was giving me a case of status anxiety; like everybody else, I wanted to be a member of the 0.1 per cent. So here I am on this gas-guzzling boat. I love the way it churns the water, love the foamy wake. The noise. The bright white carbon fibre against this deep blue background just looks so sharp.

We arrive at the more luxurious island. It's tiny. But it has a world-class wine cellar, fabulous restaurants, a pillow menu. Here, you can drink a thousand dollars' worth of wine and not be drunk. Everybody has a butler. It's as if somebody has taken the rich life of Mayfair or the Upper East Side, broken it down into its constituent parts, and rebuilt it on a tiny island in the Indian Ocean – as if rich people don't already live on a tiny island anyway. Still, you have to give them full marks for imagination.

I am led to my 'ocean bungalow' by my butler, who is silent and very respectful, which makes me feel uneasy, as always in these situations. In city hotels I usually try to take my luggage to my room myself, and if a hotel employee absolutely insists on performing the service, I stand back and let him, and then tip him: ten or twenty dollars in America, twenty euros in Europe, ten pounds in England. Once, when I was twenty-five, close to flat broke on my first foreign trip as a journalist, I checked into the Sheraton City Squire in New York and did not tip the bellboy. The bill itself had been paid by the record company of the millionaire teenage rapper I had come to interview. I was twenty-two floors up; the people and cars below were tiny. Not quite ants. But tiny. I had a shower. I got out and walked across the room. The people below were too tiny to see I was naked. Anyway, I had a towel.

My phone rang. Dripping, I picked it up.

A voice said: 'Get your clothes on, you fucking faggot.'

The line went dead.

I stood there, my face like Bob Hoskins at the end of *The Long Good Friday*, as the full horror of his situation sinks in.

Finally it sank in. The hotel had two towers. Somebody in the other tower must have seen me – somebody who could work out my phone extension by counting along the line of windows.

The bellboy I hadn't tipped.

My butler shows me around my ocean bungalow. Sitting room, bedroom, bathroom, all lushly minimalist. Bathroom with what's described as an 'oversized jacuzzi', and, among other things, a shower cubicle with four transparent walls. Outside are three terraces, two with different types of outdoor lounge furniture, one with lounge furniture plus a plunge pool. At the edge of one of the terraces is a staircase leading into the sea.

I pull out my wallet. An awkward moment, but my butler wouldn't dream of it.

Two minutes later, alone, I examine the floor of my sitting room, part of which is made of glass and actually in the sea. I'm too anxious to walk across it. So I stand at the edge and watch what's going on in Davy Jones's locker. Nothing much. My plan is to sit on the terrace in the shade, dipping my feet in the plunge pool and looking out to sea.

I will read.

A shark swims under the glass floor. Right across it! It's about three feet long. Maybe four. It's huge! Jesus, a shark. Probably a nurse shark. I am already imagining how I will tell people about the shark. The words are already forming.

Later, I sit on the terrace, mulling over the fact of the two 'ocean pavilions' a little bit along from where I am. They are either more luxurious than my ocean bungalow, or just bigger. I'm not sure which. I'm not sure which I want them to be. A party of models has recently vacated one of them, I've been told, including Kate Moss.

More luxurious, or just bigger?

If I lie on the lowest terrace, and put my head over the edge, I can look into the water and see all the fish. They are blue and yellow and orange.

Five or six little ones, the size of door keys, drift out from under a rock, then shoot back in again.

Two fish the size of stubby beer bottles are swimming around the rock in circles, trying to catch the smaller fish. But each time they swing round, the door keys shoot back in.

The stubby beer bottles go round and round, opening and closing their mouths.

Taleb says there are two worlds – the natural world, which he calls Mediocristan, and the world humans have created, which he calls Extremistan.

Mediocristan is predictable. It changes very slowly. In Mediocristan, what happened yesterday will almost certainly happen today, and again tomorrow. Fish the size of door keys will be chased by fish the size of stubby beer bottles, who will open and close their mouths. Fish the size of wine bottles will appear; they will be chased, in their turn, by fish the size of baseball bats.

This is Mediocristan. We know it well. Fish, lizards, cats and dogs. Cows, elephants. Winter, spring, summer, autumn. Mediocristan is where we used to live, before we learned to control fire, before we invented axes, spears and fish hooks. Before trade, money, science, technology.

Now we live in Extremistan. This is a place where things move very fast. Life in Extremistan is always changing. Extremistan is dominated by Black Swans. This is because the world humans have built, the world of technology and data, is complex and interconnected. When one thing changes, everything else must change along with it. Extremistan is full of cascades and avalanches. It is, incidentally, an entrepreneur's dream. It's a world that keeps breaking and reconfiguring, revealing new opportunities.

The trouble is, most of us don't understand Extremistan. We try to normalise it in our minds, by pretending we still live in Mediocristan. If we didn't do that, it would drive us nuts. In fact, it's already driving us nuts. The psychiatrist Iain McGilchrist has a brilliant theory about how the modern world, with its interlocking abstractions, is making the left sides of our brains more and more dominant over the right sides. In the past, the right brain was the boss. It was always taking snapshots of the natural world. When it needed the services of the left brain, it would feed information leftwards, via the corpus callosum, the bit that joins the two sides. Then the left brain would get to work, imagining the natural world as an abstraction, cutting it into parts, making it into tools. But then the world around us began, more and more, to resemble a product of the left brain. The world looks like tools. That's because a lot of it is made out of tools. So the left brain, the master of tools, is taking us over.

Also, Extremistan is getting more and more extreme. The scientific revolution of the 1690s made the world faster and more interconnected, and the more interconnected it became, the faster it changed, and the faster it changed, the more interconnected it became, an autocatalytic process, and now, three centuries later, money that travels from New York to London in seconds is overtaken on the way by smarter money moving many times as fast, money that buys and sells at the right price, locking in a profit, making trades in Beijing and Tokyo and Frankfurt, and getting back to Manhattan before the slow money has even crossed the water.

Our world is abstract, volatile, fragile, opaque. And therefore prone to Black Swans.

Soon, sooner than we think, something will happen, out of the blue, and it will be extreme. And then something bigger will happen, something even more extreme. An ancient ice core will melt in Greenland, and the water will seep under the Arctic ice cap, lubricating the ice, releasing an iceberg the size of Chicago, and as the iceberg melts, more ice will melt, and the planet will become less white, and so reflect less heat, and absorb more heat, which will cause more ice to melt, an autocatalytic process, a cascade, and the waters will rise, to where the tip of my nose is now, and then to the level of this terrace, and then the level of my plunge pool, and soon my ocean bungalow will disappear, the water will rise above the wooden floor and oversized jacuzzi, until the only visible thing is the top of the roof of the bigger, almost certainly more luxurious ocean pavilion a little bit along from where I am, and Kate Moss's laminated pillow menu will float away, heading in the direction of the island of plastic bottles the size of Texas.

Or maybe an algorithm will interact with another algorithm, and billions will be wiped from the economy, and entire countries will be plunged into poverty. People will die. The rich will get richer, and yet richer, and the more money they have, the more they'll want. A tipping point will be reached. Stranger things will happen.

Somebody will invent a conveyor belt that takes a rich person from his bed to the breakfast table, giving him an enema and catheterising his bladder on the way, spraying his bottom like those toilets from Japan, wafting him dry with warm air, and he won't know a thing about it until he wakes up, feeling calm and refreshed and ready for breakfast.

Right in front of me a fountain of tiny fish shoots out of the water, followed by bigger ones, and even bigger ones, all of this in two seconds, the water thrashing and churning and the fish and the water sparkling silver and blue and yellow; then all is quiet.

Something will happen. We don't have a clue what. It will turn our world upside down.

And afterwards, we'll say, well, if you think about it in this or that way, it was kind of obvious.

Which will not be true at all.

***

Back in London, I arrange to meet Nassim Taleb for the second time. I put the first time to the back of my mind.

I try to grasp the reality of Taleb. He's been called 'the world's hottest thinker'. He's one of the most influential thinkers alive.

He can really *think*, this guy.

I wish I could really think. I wish I could …

Please. Not this again.

Taleb is Lebanese, but was educated in Paris – I think the Sorbonne. Then the Wharton School, which is an Ivy League business school in Philadelphia – Warren Buffett went there, and also Donald Trump. Buffett was too clever for university, and I think that's true for Taleb, too. Talking to him, you can see that his mind moves fast and hard across the mixed terrain of dinner-table conversation. Sometimes, when he's explaining something, his right hand draws graphs in the air – there's a whole compartment of his brain that isn't just talking about something, but doing the maths as well, checking the numbers, then drawing the graphs.

He grew up outside Beirut in the 1970s. His grandfather and great-grandfather were both government ministers. His father was a scientist. The family was wealthy. Then bombs and shells started falling. They didn't stop for two decades. The Talebs left the country. They weren't nearly so wealthy any more.

As Taleb says, nobody expected the bombs and shells. They seemed to come out of the blue. Also, nobody expected them to keep coming, year after year. Everybody said, look, this will stop very soon. This will be over by Christmas. In their minds, they were living in the sort of Mediocristan in which the world behaved reasonably – the sort of place in which sudden, unexpected wars didn't happen, and if they did, they stopped before Christmas.

But Taleb – Taleb was beginning to see they were living in Extremistan.

I called his publisher. Said I'd like to meet him. They got back to me. He was in New York, where he lives. But he was coming to London. There was a lunch. I was invited. I went along. At the lunch, I either did or did not do something awful.

What Taleb totally gets is the way the modern world is all about booms and crashes. Every so often, the market booms. People join in. Then everybody wants to join in. At some point, the boom stops being rational. It's like a playground craze; I want it because you want it; I want it more because you have it. People start to behave like automatons. Their minds are gripped by mania. They can't help themselves.

Then there's a crash.

Boom and bust. Mania and panic. The world as experienced, and then described to me, by Matt Ridley. According to Matt, the general trend is up, with bumps along the way. That's Rational Optimism.

Taleb has noticed this pattern. Importantly, he's also noticed that moderation is always overpriced, and volatility is always underpriced.

There's a reason for this. Malcolm Gladwell, who always explains things beautifully, interviewed Taleb back in 2002. At this time Taleb ran a hedge fund called Empirica – so-called because he is a fan of seeing things with his own eyes, rather than relying on books and reports. Taleb invested in the stock market like a punter who only puts money on the 66–1 outsider. He would bet on a lot of outsiders, and lose money in small increments when the outsiders lost.

But occasionally the outsider would win, and Taleb would win enormous amounts of money.

Actually, it's more complex than that, because the economy is interconnected in a way that horse races are not. So when one of Taleb's outsiders won, they'd all win, as they did in the crash of 1987, or when the Russians defaulted on their debts in 1998, or when tech stocks surged and crashed around the turn of the century. People had not expected such a surge. People had not expected such a crash.

Anyway, the thing that Gladwell put so beautifully was this. He said that, given the choice, most people prefer to make small regular gains, even if this means that, once in a blue moon, they risk blowing up and losing everything. Taleb does the opposite. He makes small regular losses, and then, when something unexpected happens, he wins a huge amount of money. He's worked out that, because people can't bear to admit they don't know how the world works, he can always get better odds when he bets on unexpected events. He lives, in other words, in Extremistan.

Betting on things that seem likely feels good. Betting on things that seem unlikely feels lonely. When the unlikely thing happens, you win big. But mostly, you're losing. Mostly, you're out in the cold.

Taleb thinks the cold is the best place to be.

A while ago, trying to understand this, I became very interested in a horse bettor called Patrick Veitch who made more than a million pounds a year betting on outsiders. He had developed a method of looking at odds, and noting that sometimes the odds are wrong.

When the odds are wrong, it might mean that a 66-1 outsider has a 10 per cent chance of winning the race. So if you bet on that horse, you'll lose your money nine times out of ten. But you might make a killing on the tenth race. I say might, because nothing is certain.

What had Veitch seen? He had focused on something very specific – horse races on flat tracks over the course of a mile – and he'd seen this thing very clearly, observed its workings, and he'd devised ways of betting, even when bookmakers tried to stop him. He'd seen something others failed to see when they looked at this very specific type of horse race.

But what? Eventually Veitch agreed to meet me. I questioned him for two hours. He mentioned Taleb. Veitch had been a maths prodigy. He said he hadn't actually read Taleb, but didn't need to, because he knew he was thinking along the same lines.

He didn't tell me his secret. But I kept thinking about it. After a while, I began to understand some of its workings. It was about the difference between having a mind that sees things in a clear, unprejudiced way, and having an undisciplined mind that can't help itself, a mind that shoots off in the wrong direction and doesn't know where it's going.

Taleb's lunch was held in the Red Room, a private dining room in the Covent Garden Hotel. The hotel is smart and poised about halfway between trendy and traditional. There were, I think, six guests, as well as Taleb's publishers.

Taleb sat at the head of the table. Rory Sutherland, who people say is the smartest person in advertising, at least in London, was on the corner next to Taleb. I was next to Rory. Across from me was the broadcaster Evan Davies. There were about three professors, and Taleb's ultra-smart editor. I was wearing a corduroy jacket, with a soft collar – no lapels. It was my favourite jacket.

Taleb wore a crew-neck jersey under a tweed jacket. He sometimes says he looks like a butcher or a bodyguard – a tough guy. He does, sort of.

He was telling us about the concept of 'antifragility' – the key to his success. If something is fragile, he said, it hates volatility. It hates pretty much everything, in fact, including time. Think of a wine glass. It just wants to be left alone.

Now try to think of the opposite of that wine glass. What's the opposite of fragile? When you ask this question, most people say 'robust'. But robustness is not the opposite of fragility.

Taleb said: 'If you send a package through the mail, and you write "Fragile" on the package, you're saying: "don't harm it, don't drop it". But what would you be saying if you wrote "antifragile" on the package? You'd be asking people to harm it – you'd be saying: treat it roughly. Drop it. Kick it around.'

Something that is antifragile, in other words, is something that gains from disorder. It likes being beaten up. For instance, the human body likes exercise – when its muscle fibres are ripped and abraded, they grow back stronger. And think of the human species as a whole – we evolve because we're always being tested. Being tested makes us stronger, because the people who don't pass the test don't reproduce so much. Evolution is antifragile.

Our problem is that we don't like to evolve, because we don't like to fail. We are wedded to safety. We want to make life smooth and samey. We want to create a Mediocristan for ourselves. But that's just a fantasy. It can never happen. Our yearning for safety and predictability only makes us more fragile.

The lunch became a bit jollier. Taleb started telling a story about the British linguistic philosopher J.L. Austin. In my life, I have spent dozens of hours thinking about Austin. He had the idea that, when we say something, we are sometimes not just saying something, but also doing something. The best example of this in my life is the moment I pronounced a man guilty. One moment, he was an ex-boxer standing in the dock, having been accused of certain acts of violence. His friends and family filled the gallery. The next moment, as a result of a brief conversation between me and an older man wearing a wig, the ex-boxer's life was turned upside down. That was Austin's point – or part of it, at least. When you say things, you are also performing actions. And this guy, this pugilist – you should have seen the way he looked at me. He, too, was used to performing actions – with his fists. This was why he was in the dock in the first place. And now I was performing an action on him. Boof! An uppercut, six letters, beginning with 'g' and ending with 'y'. A knockout. At this point, the man started shouting, and so did all the people in the gallery.

Taleb's story was about a lecture given by Austin in New York, at Columbia University, in the 1950s. At the time, Austin was just about the most Oxbridge man in the world, with just about the most flinty upper-class accent it's possible to have. And there he was, telling all these Americans exactly what to think about their spoken language. There was a guy, an American philosopher called Sidney Morgenbesser, sitting right at the back of the audience.

As Taleb told the story, something lit up in my head. Ha! I knew this story! The thing about Morgenbesser was that he was a brilliant wordsmith. During the lecture, Austin made a bold pronouncement. He said that, in English, a double negative makes a positive, but that there are no languages in which the opposite is true – a double positive can never make a negative.

Taleb was getting towards the punchline, which was that Morgenbesser, in his best Bronx accent, yelled out two words across the lecture hall. He would always be known for yelling out these two words; these two words would follow him to the grave, would be the essence of his obituary.

Taleb was about to say the two words. A light went on in my head.

I genuinely don't know what happened next. Obviously, I either said the two words, ruining Taleb's story and shaming myself in front of the professors, the brilliant editor, the broadcaster and the smartest person in advertising. Or I did not say the two words. If I did not say the two words, it was because I managed to stop myself from blurting them out. If, however, I did say the two words, it was because, even though I tried to stop myself from blurting the words out, I failed.

Did I say the words? Or did I just think them?

Did my mind, against my will, force my tongue and throat to spit out two specific phonemes across the Red Room?

Seconds earlier, as Taleb was coming to the end of the Austin anecdote, I was remembering how I felt when I knocked the ex-boxer out – boof! – with my single two-syllable word.

The scene was Westminster Crown Court. A deadly serious atmosphere. As the foreman of the jury, I was standing up. The judge asked me a question: had the jury come to a unanimous verdict on either count?

The boxer, who had lost control of himself for a terrible few moments in a restaurant, was being tried on two counts. One was serious enough to put him in jail. The other was heinous – he'd go away for a long time. We had decided he was guilty of the lesser count. We were still debating the more serious one.

My first problem was that I was not expecting the judge to ask me if we had come to a verdict on *either* count. I was expecting him to ask me if we had decided on *both* counts, and I was going to say that no, we had not, and he was going to send us back for an afternoon of drinking coffee and debating the difference between, on the one hand, trying to harm someone in a specific way, and, on the other, happening to harm someone in a specific way while trying to harm them in a less specific way.

'Yes,' I said.

'Have you arrived at a unanimous verdict on count one?'

My second, much larger, problem was that I was not sure which of the offences was count one, and which was count two. Were the counts numbered in terms of escalating seriousness? Or the other way round?

The judge. The ex-boxer. The gallery containing the ex-boxer's friends and family. This was my field of vision as I racked my brains. The more I racked my brains, the more certain I was of my uncertainty.

'Yes,' I said.

The true answer to the judge's question was 'I don't know'. That's what I should have said. But something, some impulse, had forced me to say 'yes'. I had been gripped by a kind of mania. Now there was no turning back.

'How do you find the defendant?'

It was a coin-toss: 'Guilty!'

I had said something. In Austin's terms, I had also done something. The ex-boxer was shouting. The people in the gallery were shouting.

I didn't know it yet, but I'd guessed right.

Now, in the Red Room, people were laughing. I was blushing. I needed to look at Taleb's face. But I looked downwards, at my plate and cutlery. I felt hot, guilty, my mind swirling. Just like I'd felt when the ex-boxer started shouting.

***

Six weeks later, Taleb has arranged to meet me in another hotel in central London. He keeps flying back and forth across the Atlantic, on his mission to tell the human race that, even though we think we know how the world works, we don't. Our minds are designed for a more regular world than the one we have made for ourselves.

We don't live in Mediocristan any more. We live in Extremistan.

We think science is the truth. We use it to create a map of the world. We wave the map around, telling everybody we know where the treasure is buried.

But science is not the truth. Science is *provisional*. We falsify it all the time. In fact, if it can't be falsified, it's not science, as Karl Popper kept saying. Taleb loves Popper.

I sit in the lobby, drinking tea, trying to grasp the essence of Taleb's ideas – trying, to quote Taleb quoting Steve Jobs, to get my thinking clean. Jobs thought you should spend a long time getting your thinking clean. Then, when your thinking is clean, things fall into place.

I must get my thinking clean.

I sip my tea. I've poured it early, out of impatience, so it looks too milky. Anyway, one of the things Taleb lives by is the saying – coined by a friend of his who became a rabbi – that 'life is long gamma'. By long, he means 'benefits from' or 'bets on'. By gamma, he means randomness, or disorder.

Life loves randomness.

Randomness is the driver of evolution. It turned apes into us. A tiny, random mutation in the DNA of an ape – possibly a gene that relates to the corpus callosum, the heavily policed route from the left to the right hemisphere of the brain – enabled the ape to look at a forest fire, or a burning log, and think a new type of thought. Hence cooking. Hence *Homo erectus*. Hence tools, trading, money, cities, hotels. Hence the half-empty teapot on the table in front of me, the china teacup I'm holding, the milky tea.

Randomness, in Taleb's universe, is important. It's almost everything. By randomness, he means 'something we don't understand'. A random event, to Taleb, is a product of complexity – of obscure forces interacting with each other, to create changes. In the natural world – in other words, in Mediocristan – the changes happen slowly. Apes turned into us slowly. From the moment one particular ape saw a burning log and had a new type of thought to the moment a human being who was good at fishing made a deal with another human being, who was less good at fishing, to pay, in fish, for this other human being's services, say as a builder of shelters, there were 60,000 generations.

Then things started speeding up.

From that moment to the moment when Christopher Wren stood on a patch of rising land and asked his assistant Nicholas Hawksmoor to take over his building project, because he wanted to get back to London, where the action was, there were, roughly, 6,000 generations.

And from *then* – from that time of early banknotes and ships with rigging, and the world's best scientist poking himself in the eye to understand how it worked, and people having nowhere to do their laundry, and no flush toilets, even though they could build more or less perfect buildings – from *then* until the invention of the Internet, there were just twenty-nine generations.

And since the Internet happened – since Google and Facebook and YouTube and iPhones and Instagram and Snapchat and WhatsApp and Grindr and Tinder and Netflix – less than one generation.

At some point along this route, we entered Extremistan. Now algorithms are sending vast amounts of money across the Atlantic in hundredths of a second, making deals with other algorithms, creating a world we know less and less about as time goes on. Now robots are sending us messages, collecting data, performing experiments on us.

Robots are performing experiments on us? They *are*.

'How is your tea?'

I look up. It's the waitress. How is my tea? Too milky. Or rather: my tea is not strong enough, giving it the *appearance* of being too milky. Actually, strike that – it is too milky, and that's *because* it's not strong enough.

'Fine, thanks.'

Another thing Taleb swears by is Jensen's inequality, a mathematical theorem devised by the Danish mathematician Johan Jensen in 1906. Jensen's inequality is the key to what Taleb calls his 'philosopher's stone' – the *lapis philosophorum* of being antifragile, and therefore thriving in Extremistan.

I've been trying to understand Jensen's inequality for a while. It's illustrated by a convex graph, the very type of thing I understood, and then stopped understanding, at school. It's a way of expressing an analogy between, on the one hand, how evolution works, and, on the other, Taleb's method of buying options in the money markets. At least I think that's what it is. A way to make progress in a world you don't understand. Taleb says it took him twenty-five years to figure out that his trading technique – something he calls 'dynamic hedging' – is the expression of a universal pattern, a natural code. A quarter of a century of thinking – and then, bang, it fell into place.

I can grasp it, sort of. But who am I kidding? For me it hasn't *quite* fallen into place.

I must get my thinking clean.

***

And here he is. The world's hottest thinker. World leaders ask his advice.

He walks across the lobby. Bald head, trim grey beard.

I follow him downstairs to some kind of meeting room. We'll have a one-on-one talk now. Later I'll watch him talk in front of 650 people, and after that we'll go to dinner with some clever people, including Terence Kealey, the brilliant scientist who has written about how human progress is emergent, rather than planned.

Over the next few hours, Taleb will explain his ideas over and over. We live in Extremistan. We'll never understand history. In a complex system, there will be bigger deviations from the norm in the future than there were in the past. Bigger earthquakes. Bigger floods. Bigger financial crashes.

But we always build defences against the last catastrophe, never the next, that is the problem.

In the meeting room, we sit down. I want to understand Jensen's inequality – the *lapis philosophorum* that is the pinnacle of Taleb's career as a thinker, and the mathematical underpinning of his life's work.

I start off with a riff on the obesity epidemic. How it took us by surprise. How huge it is. 'We got a little bit fatter, and a little bit fatter, and then suddenly … we're off the scale.'

'My specialty is Jensen's inequality,' says Taleb. He comes *straight* out with it.

Me: 'OK!'

Taleb: 'Jensen's inequality. And what is Jensen's inequality? It tells you that anything that's convex maps into gains from variation.'

Me: 'Gains from … volatility?'

Taleb: 'From some dispersion. In other words, if you're convex to a source …'

Me: 'Um, OK.'

Taleb: 'Any convex reaction in which two is better than twice one …'

Me: 'Yes, yes.'

Taleb: 'This is a positive nonlinearity. It's convex. Then you have – automatically – gains from some variation.'

Over the next few months, I will pause the tape at this point, and draw a convex graph, and try to get my thinking clean. I will begin to see, for the second time in my life, that a curved graph is nonlinear – it describes a situation in which a small amount of one thing has a big effect on another thing. A small change makes a big difference.

OK, I will think. This is just like the convex section of the famous S-curve, the graph that describes 'phase transitions' – basically, the way everything in the universe changes from one state into another state. In his book *The Master Algorithm* the artificial intelligence expert Pedro Domingos lists some of these things: a melting ice cube, the expansion of the early universe, 'paradigm shifts in science', the way popcorn is cooked, the way you fall in love. Also, the way evolution happens in 'punctuated equilibria' – life evolves in a series of steps, or jerks, rather than a steady, linear creep.

When things change, they all seem to change in the same way. At first: nothing. Then: not much. Then: bang! – the convex part of the graph, where everything happens very quickly. Later: not much. Finally: nothing again.

The tipping point, says Domingos – the concept made famous by Malcolm Gladwell's book of the same name – might also be called the S-curve. Except 'the tipping point' is a better name. Driven by complex forces, things change slowly, and then much more quickly. Like we got a little bit fatter, and a little bit fatter … and then suddenly we're off the scale.

'So,' says Taleb, 'we are rather convex to food sources.'

We talk about diet. Taleb approves of intermittent fasting. Then we talk about: the Romans, the evolution of junk food, behavioural psychology, the behavioural psychologist Daniel Kahneman. Taleb, who reveres Kahneman, is a voracious polymath. My theory about junk food is that it must have evolved to make you hungry – in a world where the fittest survive, it's the fittest type of food. It's an *emergent* phenomenon. No planning was needed. Taleb agrees.

He agrees!

We talk about the difference, expressed in probable outcomes, between chronic and acute types of medicine. We talk about whether or not you should eat breakfast. On balance, he seems to think probably not. After all, animals in the wild need to hunt before they can eat breakfast.

'Animals run to eat,' he says. 'They don't eat to run.'

I ask him about his trip. 'This is hell. They're putting me through hell,' he says. 'Last night I couldn't sleep, so I'm sleep-deprived.' He had to get up for an early-morning TV interview. He gives talk after talk. He has said that lots of people misunderstand his talks – in fact, lots of people misunderstand his work in general. One of his main points is that randomness – luck, if you like – is important. But it's not *everything*. He never said luck was everything. That can be hard to grasp for a certain type of radio or TV interviewer.

The reality is much more subtle. If our world is becoming increasingly weird and random – which it is – we must stop trying to tame it, stop trying to control it. Don't try to negate risk. 'You can't understand it on paper,' he says.

He talks fast and uses his own patois: 'skin in the game', 'lecturing birds how to fly', the 'green lumber fallacy'. This last expression comes from a trader called Joe Siegel, who went bust. He knew a more successful trader who made lots of money trading 'green lumber', a term for unprocessed wood. This guy actually believed he was trading *wood that had been painted green*. And it didn't matter at all. The thing that mattered was that he knew how to trade it.

In this case, there were two types of knowledge. One was about the wood. The other was much more subtle and elusive. It was about the changeable amounts of money other people were prepared to pay for the wood. To the trader, the first is unimportant. The second is everything.

According to Taleb, you must make progress by tinkering – by embracing risk. Conduct small experiments; make bets you can afford to lose. Be like the early scientists. Engage with the world. Try to feel your way, always knowing that your understanding is provisional. And then, when you see an opportunity with more upside than downside – a convex graph – grab it.

You will fail often. But failure isn't shameful. You need lots of it if you're going to succeed.

We talk about Taleb's friend Aaron Brown, the famous arbiter of risk, who once told me that during the moments when he's playing poker, and during very similar moments when he's trading options in the market, he enters a certain mental state, a sort of ecstasy, and afterwards he sleeps very lightly, and has strange dreams all night.

This refers to what Taleb calls 'skin in the game'.

When you have skin in the game, you are responsible for your own losses and gains. You're a player. You are taking risks. You're truly alive. You're connected to ancient truths. Your brain is performing thousands of calculations. You're learning. You're an emergent phenomenon. You're an animal sniffing the air in the woods.

Taleb says he goes on a lot of long walks. When he has writer's block – such as the time he agreed to compress his ideas into an article for the *Wall Street Journal* – he tries not to think about the thing he can't think about.

'Don't think about it,' he says. 'Make a conscious effort not to think about it.' Eventually, your mind blurts it out.

As we talk, my mind is on the verge of blurting something out. The philosopher's stone! I can almost see it, then I can't, then it's almost there again, maddeningly close to the edge of my understanding. It's about the way things change, about the way a double negative becomes a positive, and it's connected to Patrick Veitch's horses, the growth of Starbucks, the way when I was a kid my friend Joe was mysteriously much better at fishing than me, and why that was; it's about evolution itself, tiny things having enormous effects, genes making millions of small bets, not planning anything but sometimes catching a huge wave, and riding that wave all the way from one species to the next.

I can see it!

Then I can't.

I say goodbye and shake Taleb's hand.

I can't bring myself to ask him what happened in the Red Room. Perhaps I'll never know. As I walk out of the hotel, I think about the Red Room, and a lecture hall in New York, and the philosopher Sidney Morgenbesser, and the two words he shouted across the room, and the way these two words bubbled into my head on that day six weeks ago.

The two words were: 'Yeah, yeah.'

***

Travelling to New York, pampered by corporate money, I try to think of how well off I will be for the next few days, rather than exactly why. It's easier to think of the luxury that's happening to you than the actual reason for the luxury. If you thought about the actual reason, you'd hate it.

I hate it. But I love it. I'm always glad when the Lexus or Mercedes picks me up, I always enjoy the smooth ride to the airport, the leather seats, the normally self-effacing driver, the *chauffeur*.

Sliding into the polished animal-skin interior I remember a recent chauffeur, not self-effacing, Russian, who, when I got in the car, asked me if I wanted a massage.

'Do you want massage?'

'No!'

And then: 'Uh, no *thank* you.'

'I show you massage.'

The Russian did not leave his seat. He flicked a few buttons. The leather beneath my butt and back began to undulate.

Driven by a chauffeur, you see the *point* of a motorway. Fast-tracked to the first-class lounge, you don't mind the mild drag of passport control. In the lounge, you are grateful for the range of food unavailable in the rest of the airport – food for the ascetic, rather than the hungry or the greedy. Rich people like the quinoa and kale, and if they don't, they still like to see it around.

In any case, when you get on the plane, there is always someone who has a better seat, or even a better type of seat, than you. You feel a twinge of pique that you're not at the absolute front of the plane; the person who is at the absolute front of the plane is simultaneously experiencing a twinge of pique that he's not in a private jet. The man in the private jet is piqued that it's not *his* private jet. The man who owns a private jet wishes it was a *bigger* private jet.

I try to settle in my seat. I think I'm in some kind of *premium business class*.

Recently, I wrote a story about the non-human passengers who had been detained at the airport. They didn't have proper credentials. I went to visit them in their holding facility. Young crocodiles, some huge dragon-like monitor lizards and a boa constrictor, among other things. The monitor lizards had been on their way to an address in Mexico – one doesn't know for sure, but maybe the home of a rich drug baron, who had not come forward to claim them. So these ferocious things remained in limbo, whipping their tails around. A flick from that tail could break someone's leg, I was told, which made me think a bit more about the drug baron and his lifestyle.

Arriving in New York, there's the moment when I see the forest of towers from the bridge, and as always I get a strong sense of a crowd of people packed in a tiny space, a small island; everybody has come to the small island to look for something, and they built all these towers, so they must have found what they were looking for.

For me, this time it's models. The time before, it was starlets. I can't remember the last time I wrote about a woman who was not beautiful. On the other hand, I can't remember the last time I wrote about a man who was not a hard-driving obsessive – which means I am helping to promote a fantasy world of obsessive men and beautiful women.

My hotel has been refitted and is now more upmarket than when I last stayed here. It's gone from classic to edgy. The walls are hung with art by the sort of artist who, if you asked him to draw a picture for you, would draw a picture of a penis. Not the *sort* of artist who would draw a penis – the actual artist. In fact an ejaculating penis. Which is, if you think about it, pretty profound. I loved his diamond-encrusted skull, by the way. It's money, it's *about* money; it's about death, it *is* death. His penis – which I'm proud to own – is obscene, yes, but human life can't exist without it. In my room, there's a sinister-looking picture of a rabbit by I think Julian Schnabel. The furniture might be in a Marilyn Manson video – dark velvet things and so on. The bathroom products are by Aesop. The floorboards are varnished red oak. There is an excellent universal adaptor for any of my own appliances if I want to use them. The shower is complex and also powerful. Dark towers crowd the sky outside my window. Margaret Atwood is staying here. I saw her checking in.

I have my mornings and evenings off, but every afternoon, for three days in a row, I will be interviewing three models – that is, nine models in all. Adriana Lima, Raquel Zimmerman, Isabeli Fontana, Gigi Hadid, Natalia Vodianova, Sasha Luss, Joan Smalls, Carolyn Murphy, Karen Elson. They make between one and seven million dollars a year, which means, given that the fashion industry's profit margin is about 10 per cent, that they're expected to generate sales of something like half a billion dollars a year between them. There is something specific about the way they look that makes women want to buy clothes and beauty products. They have been through a rigorous selection process which filters the faces and bodies of thousands of women until only a few are left. These are the ones who are believed to trigger a precise set of drives in the minds of female consumers. They are the product of the female gaze, the increasingly lucrative female gaze.

The models are tall, extremely slender, extremely feminine, and very young-looking for their age. They are photogenic, which means that they look at their best when reduced to pixels – the sort of reduction that coarsens and dumpifies a typical face. The models have high cheekbones, which makes them look slightly feline, or aristocratic, or even haughty. They have features that, in a resting position, look as if their owners believe themselves deserving of special treatment. They are women who project a significant degree of girlishness. They can look racy in expensive, demure clothes, just as they can look dignified in underwear. When they walk, a precise geometry of hip and thigh proclaims their femininity.

In many people, images of these models arouse anger, and when you analyse this anger, it's really about the power of the images – the power they have to hurt people, to make people feel unworthy and inadequate.

I spend the morning in my room, looking at pictures of models, thinking about models, lounging on the interesting furniture. I go for a walk in the slanting sunlight and buy a tiny bottle of ginger juice at a juice bar for a sum of money that would feed a Bangladeshi seamstress for a week. Then I go back to my junior suite or whatever it is and think about what it would be like if I had a home with a big art deco-style sink, and a toilet with a classic 'American flush'. You can order these toilets online; at some point in the future, I tell myself, I will do just that.

A black SUV, I think a Chevrolet Suburban, picks me up and takes me to the studio, which is a former warehouse in the meatpacking district. I take an industrial lift to an enormous room whose previous life I try to imagine. The ranks of carcasses, the chains and hooks. Now it's a lounge with lovely velvet sofas and coffee tables and side tables with a buffet. The buffet will be updated every few hours, according to the time of day. Now it's perfect egg sandwiches with capers, cut into thin slices and stacked so the capers look like beads, the whole thing like a geometric design. There are raspberry and blueberry pies with latticework pastry, and kale-based smoothies in artisan-looking bottles, arranged in wicker baskets. Most of the buffet will leave the room uneaten, and in four days' time the lovely sofas and tables will go back to the rental agency and this industrial space will be bare again.

The models are posing for a calendar sponsored by a tyre company. I interview them, one by one, mostly on a leather sofa, after they have been photographed by Steven Meisel. It is made clear to me that Meisel, who is credited with inventing the concept of the supermodel in the 1980s, and who is famous for taking the pictures for Madonna's book *Sex*, will not speak to me. He is in one room, photographing the models. Then they talk to me. Meisel's talent is that he can make female faces look dramatic and full of desire, smoky-eyed and full-lipped, with flared nostrils; they want something so much they're absolutely bursting, but they are so beautiful, so fine of feature, so rarefied and singular, that their greed is dignified, their petulance forgiven.

The point of view is not male or female, not his or hers. It's money's.

They tell me about their lives while I take photographs of them with my smartphone. They mostly have similar stories. They were not beautiful as teenagers. They were skinny. As teenagers, they were not the hot girls. Then somebody spotted them – the thin wrists and ankles, the internal scaffolding of the face. The tiny margins that make all the money. Now they fly across the globe, taking advantage of their ten or fifteen years at the top. 'My travelling's been crazy,' says Lima. She has split up with the father of her two daughters. 'When you are a mother,' she says, 'you are constantly guilty.' Zimmerman tells me she deals with the modelling life with

Transcendental Meditation: 'It's very easy. Just relax. Close your eyes. And then … you let go.'

They are slim but not skinny. That's the whole point. Hadid has slender arms and legs and a youthful face; many people could have limbs like hers, at the expense of their faces, or vice versa. In a conversation I have with Vodianova and a few other people, she says: 'We are models. We are constantly asked this question: how do you do it? Well, you know, it's in our genes. That's why we're in the profession in the first place.'

They love dressing up. They talk about shoes. The thing about shoes, Smalls tells me, is that shoes are just a small detail, but they can transform your whole look. Murphy says: 'As Tom Ford told me, the reason women wear high heels, and I still don't know if he was yanking my chain, he had seen something about baboons, and the female baboon, when she would stand up on her toes, it was almost like a mating call, and it would send the male baboons into this frenzy.'

Hadid says: 'I actually am obsessed with shoes.' Thinking about high heels, she says: 'They are shit to wear. They're horrible to wear. They're so uncomfortable. But they're cute to look at.'

She looks at me. 'Beauty is pain,' she says.

I go for a long walk. I think about something Fontana said to me: 'The world wants to look at women. Women want to look at women. Men want to look at women.' I go back to the luxury of my hotel – the edgy art, the American flush. I have one more day of this. Then it's back to being a guy who is not rich, who wishes he was rich, who spent most of his life feeling guilty about wishing he was rich.

And in the car on the way to the airport, in the airport itself, and in the plane, where I have a tiny little bed, the sort of luxury a field officer might be afforded in combat, I think of the reason for this luxury. As I snuggle down on my mattress, thin but miraculous in these circumstances, in this slightly rank steel tube, feeling the bumpy sky knocking at my bones, I work it out logically. It's because I've interviewed the photogenic women. It's because pictures of the photogenic women will be in the magazine.

It's because men want to look at women. It's because women want to look at women. It's because, when women look at a certain type of woman, money is made. It's because of the female gaze, the lucrative female gaze. It's because of an exact type of beauty that is a magnet for money. It's because beauty is pain. It's because of the sheer focused genius of Steven Meisel. It's because the sheer focused genius of Steven Meisel will sell tyres. It's because I will sell tyres, I'm thinking as my head sinks into my tiny pillow.

***

I go to a Jordan Belfort seminar, to watch Belfort in person; he will teach a group of people, each of whom have paid £600, how to get rich. Belfort is now a global brand. Since the Scorsese film came out, almost everybody you speak to knows who you mean when you say 'the Wolf of Wall Street'.

The Wolf of Wall Street. The guy who is simultaneously in two images. In one he is surrounded by wealth – the yacht, the helicopter, the bundles of cash. The picture of success. In the other he is surrounded by wealth – the yacht, the helicopter, the bundles of cash. The man destroyed by money.

The movie, by the way, is great. It leads you along the fault-line in your own head, the conflict you always had; it's an exposé of greed, and also an enactment of the thing it's exposing. It's a wicked film, taking you by the hand and leading you towards an understanding of your own filthy materialism, and then persuading you to revel in that materialism. Scorsese delivers dopamine hit after dopamine hit – in scene after scene, he shows you what a Faustian pact is actually like, the pieces of it, the tawny-pink flesh, the country pile, the porn mansion, the white of the boat and the blue of the sea and the crispness of the suits and the bubbles in the champagne; it's what you want but it's really nothing, and it hurts you, damages your mind so in the end it's less than nothing, it's anti-value, and even when you know all this you're still laughing, still hopped up, still excited to the point of mania – you still want it, by God, because, like everybody, you are a pirate, and when there is buried treasure to be had, you will drop everything and go to the ends of the earth to find that buried treasure; you might try to deny it but you know it's true.

That's the society we live in. That's who we are. We seek the treasure; we love the treasure. We are ruined. Not by the treasure, but by our *love* of the treasure.

In the final scene, Scorsese shows us Belfort, on stage, giving a seminar, teaching people how to be rich, and the camera swings away from Belfort and shows us the audience, rows and rows of people sitting there, staring ahead, absolutely transfixed, and it takes a couple of seconds to realise what this means, what he is telling us.

He's showing us ourselves.

That's us up there.

That's me.

The monster.

***

I'm trying to work out how many people must be in this audience. A couple of thousand at least – which at £600 each equals, let's see, over £1 million. I've got a Platinum ticket, but there's a whole group closer to the stage, and they all have personal *desks* – the Diamond ticket-holders. They must be paying more.

Belfort can get an audience on this scale all over the world, and frequently does; hundreds of thousands of people want to see him.

Why?

Because they believe in him. They think he will help them get rich.

What do I think?

I think they're right. I know how people get rich. True, I'm not rich myself. But I know *how* people get rich. I could get up on that stage myself, and tell these people how to get rich. I *could*. I definitely could.

In my mind, I walk across the stage. Loud music? Yes. 'I've Gotta Feeling', by the Black Eyed Peas? Possibly. I don't see why not. It's about going out and getting blasted, so the message is wrong. That's a reason why not. One of the main things I'd want to say to these people, one of my main messages, would be: stop going out and getting blasted!

The song is there to grab your attention.

So now I look at the audience. All these people who want to get rich, who are not rich, who have saved up their money and spent it on motivation. You have to bear that in mind. I will walk up and down and *motivate* them. I've always wanted to be a motivational speaker. One day I'll write a book about a motivational speaker whose life is falling apart. What a very good idea indeed that is, by the way.

My style: quipping, but controlled – like the late, great Jim Rohn. Jim would often quote the Bible. He used to pick out certain words and say them in a slightly higher voice. Very effective. Jim was slick as anything. Slicker than the guys who came after him, who cited him. Anthony Robbins, slick but also a powerhouse. I was once in a Robbins audience, and he wanted us to walk in bare feet on hot embers while chanting the words 'Cool moss!' I hid in the upper gallery, and then came out and watched the whole thing, the fire-walking, and saw how it worked.

Anyway, Jim. Jim would say: 'Ask and you shall receive.' There's more to that sentence than you might think, by the way.

So I'd be a bit like Jim. Also, I'd want to be backed by music all the way through. Something soft and thoughtful, strings being plucked, the strings picking out the emotion in my words.

I'd start out speaking softly.

I remember when I was a kid, I'd say. I used to go fishing with this other kid, I'd say. He was called Joe.

Joe was my best friend.

In the summer, the two of us would go fishing every day. We found this special place where we could fish for bass. And every day, we'd bring home four or five good-sized bass.

If we brought home five bass, Joe would have caught four of them. If we brought home four, he would have caught all four. I sometimes caught one. A lot of the time I caught nothing.

Every so often I'd ask Joe what he did that was different to what I did. We used the same sort of rods and reels, the same sort of lures and baits. He said he didn't know what he did differently, because he didn't know exactly what I was doing. He just knew what *he* was doing. Sometimes he'd catch three big fish, one after the other, in what seemed like no time. He must have a trick, I imagined. A short cut. A secret I didn't know about.

The whole thing bothered me for a while. But then we got older and went our separate ways. There was always this mystery somewhere at the back of my mind. What had I not seen?

Well, I never thought I'd solve that mystery.

Later in life, a lot of people I knew did well financially. They got rich. I did not get rich. Sure, I had little bits of success here and there, and if you looked at it in a certain way, it looked OK. But every time I got some money, it would just shrink away, and then I'd be poor for a while.

It's not as if I didn't do any work. I did do some work. And sometimes I got results. But I could never seem to turn those results into real wealth. Some people could. I couldn't. I figured I was just one of those people who couldn't.

One day I met this guy who could make money – Patrick Veitch. If you met Veitch, you'd think he was a very precise type of guy – somebody who thinks very cleanly. Talking to him, you'd feel like a slob. He gets the point of everything immediately. He makes distinctions and connections. A man with a fine mind. He passed the entrance exam to read maths at Cambridge when he was sixteen.

Veitch studied horses. He applied his analytical brain. He studied 100 hours a week. Week after week. He watched races. He collected data, and he'd look at the data, and make predictions, and then update his thinking, and look for more data, and update his thinking again. He became a relentless learning machine, tuning his brain to the finest of details, the smallest of margins.

Then ... he saw something in the data.

What happened next? Veitch started making bets. He acted. In the first ten weeks, he won £338,000. A good portion of this money was due to the thing he'd seen in the data. He wasn't always right. He backed some losers. He backed a couple of outsiders who came a close second, but only because the jockey had performed particularly badly. And those two horses went on to win more races, and the horses that had narrowly beaten them faded away.

He had looked at the data. He had seen something valuable. Years later, it's still valuable. Now he wins a million pounds a year.

Veitch had seen a trick. He would not tell me what it was.

One day I was talking to a former professional gambler from Los Angeles named Josh Axelrad. Josh had been a member of a team of blackjack card-counters. He made hundreds of thousands of dollars in casinos – Las Vegas, Reno, Atlantic City. Josh took me to a casino so he could show me how card-counting works.

Blackjack is pretty simple. Everybody, including the dealer, gets two cards, and everybody can ask the dealer for more cards. The object is to get the numbers on your cards to add up to twenty-one or as close to twenty-one as possible. Cards with pictures count as ten. If you go over twenty-one, you're bust. If the dealer goes over twenty-one, he's bust.

Under normal circumstances, the dealer has a slight edge. That's because he plays his hand last. If you go bust as you're chasing twenty-one, he does not have to bet. This slight edge means that, if the game were to progress indefinitely, the casino would end up with all the chips, and the players would end up with nothing.

But there's something you can do to reverse this situation – to give yourself a slight edge over the dealer. In the 1960s, a mathematician called Ed Thorp worked it out. He saw that low cards – two, three, four, five and six – slightly favour the dealer. High cards, on the other hand – the tens, pictures, and aces – slightly favour the player. Sevens, eights and nines are neutral. High cards favour the player for several reasons. One is that, if the dealer gets sixteen or less, he is obliged to take another card. Another is that the player is allowed to split his cards, and double his bets – 'doubling down'.

So here's what you do. If you count the cards as they arrive on the table, giving each low card a value of one, and each high card a value of minus one, the running tally gives you an account of the ratio of low cards to high cards that have already been played. Therefore, it also gives you a running tally of the ratio of low cards to high cards that have yet to be played.

When the count is low, the deck favours the dealer. But when the count is high – bang! That's the time to raise your bets.

What was Axelrad doing? He was looking inside the deck. He did not have a perfect view; he could only see what was in the deck by looking at what *wasn't* in the deck. And in order to find out what *wasn't* in the deck, he needed to make lots of small bets, and while he was making these small bets, the dealer had a slight edge.

And while the dealer had a slight edge, Axelrad was slowly losing money. But as his money was bleeding away, he was collecting data. He was learning.

And then – bang!

Most data is 'noise'. It doesn't tell you anything you want to know. But sometimes you see a signal in the noise.

Patrick Veitch looked at data about horses, and saw a signal in the noise.

Patrick wanted to understand a specific thing about a specific type of horse. Joe wanted to understand a specific thing about a specific type of fish. He wanted to see inside the water, just like Josh wanted to see inside the pack of cards.

Patrick, Joe and Josh – they all discovered a trick.

I was talking to a writer called Matthew Syed. And he made me grasp something very important about these tricks.

What he told me was about tennis.

Syed used to be a champion table-tennis player. He played ping-pong. He represented Great Britain at the Olympics.

But one day, he was playing tennis – not ping-pong, but tennis – at a charity event. He was up against the former Wimbledon champion Michael Stich.

Stich was famous for his killer serve.

Syed told Stich not to hold back. Just do your normal serve, he said.

Stich threw the ball in the air and lifted his racket. Syed waited for him to hit the ball.

He waited and waited.

Stich wondered what was going on. He'd served at Syed. But Syed had not moved.

Syed hadn't seen the ball.

Stich served again. Again, Syed did not move. Again, he hadn't seen the ball. He was waiting for it. He was looking for it. But he just couldn't see it. The first thing he knew about Stich's serves was when the balls hit the canvas behind him.

If this happened to you, you'd think: well, this kind of makes sense. You'd think your reactions weren't quick enough. But the thing about Syed was that he was a table-tennis champion. His reactions *were* quick enough. Whenever somebody served a ping-pong ball at him, he had a quarter of a second to react.

Stich's serves were slower than that. It took *half* a second for Stich's serves to cross the court.

Syed went to see a professor of motor behaviour. He was fitted with an eye-tracking device. He stood in front of a screen, and on the screen was a tennis player serving at the camera.

The professor told Syed what had been happening. He'd been looking in the wrong place. A novice looks at the ball. A middling player looks at the arc of his opponent's serving arm. But professional players don't look at the serving arm, because it moves too fast.

Professionals look at the area around the server's hips. If you were to track Roger Federer's eyes, that's where he'd be looking. At the server's hips. That's where the rich data is. When you play against a fast opponent, you have to look at his hips. But it takes time. It takes years of practice. But then the wiring of your brain changes.

Just like when you were a kid, when you stopped looking at the ball, and started looking at the arc of the server's arm. The wiring of your brain changed then, too.

Now, I'm standing on this stage looking out at all of you, and I know why you're here. You want to get rich. You're not rich, but you want to get rich. And I can see a lot of you are in your thirties, and some of you are in your forties. So I'm guessing you've tried to get rich, but you're not rich, and that's why you're here.

You've tried. But it hasn't worked. It hasn't stuck. Hasn't taken off. You always feel like you're missing the big opportunity. You're missing the trick. You're not catching the big fish. You're not getting the big wins.

Do you feel like life is a casino, and the casino always has the edge? Sure, it's only a slight edge. It's not so big that you stop playing. Because that's what casinos always do, right? They keep you playing. And every day, you bleed a bit more, and you go home. And the next day you go back into the casino, and bleed a bit more.

Do you sometimes feel like you're playing tennis, and you can't see the ball? The ball just whizzes past you, and the first thing you know is the sound – the *whack* of the ball when it hits the canvas behind you. And when this happens again and again, what do you want to do?

You want to stop playing, right? Because there's a limit to the number of times you can hear that sound.

That whack.

You know, I once had a conversation with a famous surgeon. He's called Atul Gawande. He's one of the best-known doctors in the world. A great surgeon. He once wrote that, in his profession, you know you're at the top of your game when somebody says: 'You're a machine, Gawande.'

But what happens when you perform your first operation? Gawande says that when he did his first operation, he was academically prepared. He knew his anatomy books. He'd practised on the dead bodies of people who donated their bodies to science. And he'd also performed mock operations on latex models of body parts.

This first operation was very simple. He just had to reach inside somebody's ribcage and put a stitch into some connective tissue. That was it. So he put his gloves on. He reached inside. And he couldn't do it.

He couldn't do it because inside the chest cavity ... it felt all wrong. The person's living body did not have the exact dimensions he'd imagined from the models and the books.

He tried again. He failed again. He was sticking the needle in the wrong place.

He kept trying. He moved further in and felt around. And then, finally, he got it.

The next time he was better. The time after that he was better still.

Now he's a machine.

So: how do you get to be a machine? Well, you have to study. But there comes a point when you can't learn anything more without actually *doing* something. You can't move forward without performing an *action*. Imagine you're stuck on a ledge, like the climber Joe Simpson. He smashed his knee up, it was like a bag of bone fragments, and he fell into a crevasse. He didn't die because his fall was broken by a huge plug of snow. And he found himself on a ledge. He knew, for sure, that if he stayed on that ledge, he would die. And he looked up, and saw that the walls of the ravine were made of ice. His knee didn't work. So he couldn't go up.

He had two choices. Stay on the ledge and die. Or lower himself into the ravine. Into the unknown. Into the void. Knowing that if you don't find anything down there before you get to the end of your rope, you'll be too weak to climb back up.

And how do we know this story? Because Joe Simpson did not stay on the ledge.

He entered the void. He discovered something about the void. He discovered an ice bridge that led him, eventually, after a long struggle, to safety.

At first, the ledge might look like the safest option. But it's not. It's the most dangerous option. You can't learn anything on the ledge. On the ledge, all you can do is die.

So: there are two states of mind. There's thinking. And then there's acting. You need to think. But you also need to act. Patrick Veitch has a term for this dichotomy. He calls it 'the Brain Surgeon and the Mad Axeman'. You must be both of these things at once. You need to know your stuff, but you need to make forceful, confident decisions. Think about what a decision is. It comes from the Latin word meaning 'to cut'. When you make a decision, you're making a cut. You're cutting something off.

I'd say this: it's not about knowing your stuff, and then making decisions. In *order* to know your stuff, you need to make decisions. I'd say this: you only really know your stuff *when* you start to make those decisions – those cuts.

Those cuts are a risk. You're taking a risk. And I've talked to a lot of people who got rich. And there's one thing that separates them from the rest of the population.

They know they need to take that risk. You might say they relish that risk. When they cut into the world, they know the cut needs to be very precise. Tiny margins are everything.

But they know they need to make that cut.

I talked to Howard Schultz. He made that cut. He saw that if you made coffee shops a bit more comfortable, people would spend more time in those coffee shops. They'd hang out in those coffee shops. They'd spend money like people spend money in bars. So he took a risk, and opened a coffee shop. He filled the coffee shop with comfortable chairs and sofas. He called it Starbucks.

I talked to Felix Dennis. He made that cut. He saw a bunch of guys lining up to watch a Bruce Lee film. And he realised that these guys had nowhere to go if they wanted Bruce Lee merchandise. Like posters. These were not the sort of guys who went into upmarket poster shops. So Dennis worked out what to do. He worked out every step in the process. He'd create a Bruce Lee poster, and fold it up so it was the size of a magazine, and sell it in newsagents. Because these Bruce Lee fans did go into newsagents.

The comfortable chairs. The folded posters. Little things that made a big difference.

Dennis acted. And, as he acted, he learned. Beyond a certain point, you can't learn any more without doing things. And when you start doing things, what will happen? You'll do them wrong. But then you'll do them a bit less wrong, and a bit less wrong.

Nassim Taleb is one of the most famous traders in the world. In fact, he made so much money he stopped trading. What he says is that when you learn, you evolve. In other words, learning is a process of getting rid of bad ideas, in the same way that evolution is a process of killing off the life forms that are less fit.

It's a battle royale. You must kill off all your bad ideas until what you're left with is the one good idea – the idea that works.

He also said that we live in a time of great market volatility. But most people don't believe in this volatility; they don't want to believe in it. Most people want to believe the world is more stable than it is. But we live in a world of bubbles and crashes. We live in a world where unexpected things happen much more often than we think they do.

Learn how to bet, says Taleb. Feel your way into the market. Put your skin in the game. At first, you'll lose. But one day, you'll see an opportunity. You'll see a 66-1 outsider. You'll see a deck stacked with tens and aces and kings and queens.

You'll look at the water, and you'll cast your line out, and you'll catch those bass.

I guess you'll want to know if I ever found out what Veitch was actually doing. And the answer is: I don't know. I'll never know. But I think it was all about how some young horses, a very small percentage, become great in a very short time. They reach a kind of tipping point, maybe around their second birthday. One day, it takes them sixty-three seconds to run a mile. A couple of months later, they can do it in fifty-seven seconds.

If you're a tennis player, you might go from being a solid player on the tour to a Federer or an Agassi, and this transformation will happen in a couple of years. With a horse, it happens much more suddenly. And if you collect hundreds of data points from those few weeks, from a pool of hundreds of horses, you can run that data through a simple neural network – 'back-propagate' the data – and what you'll see, with a great horse, is an S-curve. A convex graph. A curved line denoting a period of exponential change. And what you *then* do, you study the early part of the graph, so you can pick up on the horse's exponential rise as soon as possible, so you know the horse is great before anybody else does.

Is this what Veitch does? I don't know. But maybe he does something like that. If you look at any great success, you'll see a convex graph. You'll see an S-curve, a tipping point. You just have to work out what happens *before* the tipping point.

And what was I doing wrong all those years ago, when we were fishing for bass? And what was Joe doing right? I was making casts, and winding my lure in, and making more casts. Sometimes – very occasionally – I got lucky.

But Joe was working the water. He was learning something new with every cast. He imagined the water in front of him, within his casting range, as a big cubic space, and he covered that space, letting the lure drop a bit, going from deep to shallow, zigging left to right a little. He couldn't see inside the cube, but he could imagine what was inside the cube, and sometimes, he'd realise where the fish were, how they were moving through the water.

That's all it was. But it was the most important thing. Whatever you're doing, there's a three-dimensional space in front of you. And you need to enter this space. You need to move through this space. You need to find the right path. And, in order to find the right path, you need to take the wrong path, over and over.

But think about that wrong path, and what it really is. It's one of the bad ideas you discard before you find the good idea. It's part of the learning process. It's evolution in action.

In fact, without taking the wrong path, you would never be able to recognise the right path.

So take the wrong path. It's the only way to find the right path. Ask and you shall receive. But the thing is: you have to keep asking.

Are you beginning to see the trick? Let me tell you about a writer called Steven Pressfield. He wrote one of the best books on this subject.

It's called *The War of Art*.

I would tie it in first place with *The Slight Edge*, by Jeff Olsen, if any of you have heard of that book. Pressfield and Olsen understand the trick with perfect clarity.

Pressfield is a writer. He writes historical novels, particularly about Spartan warriors. Anyway, he spent many years *wanting* to be a writer without actually *being* a writer. Something was standing in his way. Something was stopping him. Some powerful force. He calls the force resistance.

'Most of us have two lives,' he says. 'The life we live, and the unlived life within us. Between the two stands resistance.'

What is resistance? It's the force that stops you. You might want to be a painter, or a film director, or a novelist. You might want to start a school for kids with learning difficulties. You might want to produce a gangster film, or start a business buying time from poor people and selling it to rich people. You might want to put your dirty bed in an exhibition in a gallery, and then sell it for millions, or encrust a dead person's skull with diamonds.

What's stopping you from doing these things? Resistance.

So what is resistance? It's 'the most toxic force on the planet'. It's the force that stops you from doing what you want to do. It's inside your head. It will do anything to stop you from sitting at your desk and writing, to stop you picking up the phone and making that call. It will drive you to drink, to drugs, to parties, to lying in bed doing nothing. It will make you depressed and anxious. It makes us feel sick. It gives us headaches. It makes us doubt and sabotage ourselves.

'It will reason with you like a lawyer or jam a nine-millimetre in your face like a stick-up man,' says Pressfield.

It's hard to sit at your desk, and try to write, and fail, and try again, and fail again. It's much easier to do almost anything else. It's easier to stay in bed. It's easier to wander around with no particular destination in mind. It's easier to go to the nearest smelly bar.

The thing that's hard is thinking. The thing that's hard is thinking clearly. It's easier to do almost anything than it is to think clearly.

But if you take the hard choice, says Pressfield, if you get your thoughts clear, if you think, hard, every day, and act on your thoughts, something magical happens.

It won't happen today. It won't happen tomorrow. It might not happen for years. But it will happen.

If you take the hard choice, over and over, if you think and act, every day, you will learn things. And those things will add up. They will compound, like interest.

Think of yourself as a currency. Every time you learn something, you're adding value to that currency. For a long time, you won't notice the added value. That's why most people quit. The added value takes a long time to arrive.

Most people walk away before that point.

Most people quit.

But if you make the hard choice, over and over, your value will start to compound. One day you'll hit an S-curve.

One day you'll find yourself ahead of the game. You'll be getting paid for something nobody else even thought of selling. You'll be Tom Sawyer.

That's the trick.

You'll find the right path. You'll find the right path by taking many wrong paths.

That's the trick.

There is a force that wants you to be poor. It lives inside you. It is you. Kill it. That's the trick.

What happens when you find the right path? You find yourself catching the big fish. You win the big bets. You break your opponent's serve. You suddenly find the casino of life no longer has the edge over you.

Now you have the edge over the casino.

Take the hard choice. Think clearly. Try and fail. Try again and fail again. Act and learn. Be the brain surgeon and the mad axeman. You have to be both.

Ask and you shall receive. Ask again. Ask a thousand times.

That's the trick.

Thank you.

***

Belfort arrives on the stage. Black suit, no tie, white shirt, black shoes. He strides and gesticulates. The Queens accent comes across very strongly. He tells us about the nature of getting rich. He believes you always get rich quickly. You have to focus on putting the puzzle together. But then, when you've put the puzzle together, the money pours in quickly. If we're not rich, it's because we have capitulated to the force that wants to make us average.

We are actively *stopping ourselves* from being rich.

'I've been a rich man and a poor man,' he says, 'and I choose rich every time.'

Look at the person on your left, he says. The person on my right looks at me. One day, says Belfort, you'll pull up at the traffic lights, and this is the person you'll see next to you. And this person will be driving a Porsche. The guy next to me smiles. There is nobody to the left of me, because I'm next to the aisle.

There are two types of people, he says. Ducks and eagles. Eagles soar. 'Ducks waddle around in duck shit. And you know what? There's not a single duck in the room. Ducks don't come to these rooms.'

Belfort tells us his life story. How he was going to be a dentist, but dropped out of dental school. How he discovered selling. He sold ice cream, then meat and fish, then financial products.

On an enormous screen above the stage, Belfort plays a clip from the Scorsese film in which Leonardo diCaprio plays the young Belfort. In the clip, Belfort is a young broker working at Investors' Center, the crummy office where sleazy guys sell cheap stocks to people without much money – 'selling garbage to garbage men', as he will say later.

We watch as diCaprio's young Belfort uses the Straight Line to persuade a guy called John to part with $4,000. All the sales techniques are there – the 'language patterns', the lowered voice, which denotes scarcity, the harvesting of micro-assent, the rhythmic waves of certainty, the change of pace, the capturing of attention. As the pitch increases in momentum, the schlumpy guys in the office turn their heads. Then they stop what they're doing. They begin to huddle around diCaprio.

DiCaprio tells John: 'Your profit on a mere six thousand dollar investment could be upwards of sixty thousand dollars.' As he says this, he's punching the air.

He locks in the sale. Everybody in the room applauds him – the thirty-something and forty-something guys in their open-necked shirts and slacks. 'The other guys looked at me like I just discovered fire,' says diCaprio.

The clip ends. Everybody in the auditorium applauds. Belfort continues with his talk, which is actually a pitch. All the sales techniques are here – the raised and lowered voice, the rhythmic waves of certainty, the changes of pace, the capturing of attention.

At the end of the afternoon, I'm feeling hopped up, optimistic, high on dopamine. Belfort tells us he has an offer to make us. The offer is another seminar – a better one, more exclusive, more valuable. The seminar costs £1,500. He tells us that people have gathered at the side of the auditorium, and they are holding credit card readers. We have to stay in our seats until he says so. The seminar is limited to a small number of people. Not all of us will be lucky.

He gives the order. Hundreds of people rush to the side of the auditorium. Queues form in front of the card readers.

Another sale locked in. Belfort walks off the stage. The money pours in quickly.

Coda

The plane takes off and heads north, towards the snow and ice, towards the discomfort. I have packed thermal underclothes and waterproof overclothes. We angle upwards and bump through some clouds, and then we're in the clear night air.

It's dark outside the window. I can see myself, half in shadow, a face at the window, until I pull the blind down.

***

I went to see Felix Dennis a second time. He'd recently been treated for cancer of the throat.

When I got to his garden there were some new statues – a bronze gorilla, based on King Kong, and a life-size statue of a woolly mammoth, being hunted by a tribe of what looked like *Homo habilis*, the apes who discovered fire. Dennis called them 'people before people'. They were small and furious-looking. One was frozen in the act of hurling a rock.

I walked past the statue of Icarus meeting his fate, poised above the pond, his head inches from the water. Outside the Welshman's was a new statue, life-size, of Isambard Kingdom Brunel, wearing a top hat and smoking a cigar. The most industrious man in history, welcoming you to your study.

Dennis was in the Welshman's, sitting at his desk. We talked about his life. It was based on two revelations. The first, that he could make money, came at the age of twenty-four. He became obsessed. He developed a one-track mind. 'You've got to go straight after it,' he said. 'As soon as I saw what happened with my Bruce Lee poster magazines, I then started to look at other movies. I saw this shark. Other people just saw a shark movie. I didn't. I saw money.'

The shark movie was *Jaws*. Dennis made millions selling pictures of a rubber shark. He didn't care how he made money – as long as it was legal. He just wanted the money.

'If I'd been making contact lenses,' he said, 'I'd have found a way of making money.'

Dennis made £500 million. But the money, or the mindset he had to adopt to make the money, or the peculiar way people treated him when he had the money, or the emotional hardness he developed to deal with those people, or the drugs he took to forget about this hardened person he'd become, who he didn't particularly like, who he thought of as a 'shit' – all of these things began to poison him. He became depressed and ill. Night after night, he hired prostitutes for company. He constantly smoked crack.

At the age of fifty he nearly died.

Soon after that, he had his second revelation. He was, he said, 'a rich, successful idiot. Nearly everybody who makes a lot of money, they're nearly all idiots. They're nearly all mad. Because they think they're immortal. You are a bit mad. You're pretty close to madness.'

He paused. 'For me, discovering that I could write poetry – and I will admit, I will go further, discovering that I could write poetry that other people would read and listen to – completely transformed my life.'

Poetry was the second revelation. Dennis became obsessed with it. Lines of poetry kept appearing in his head.

'I wake up in the middle of the night, virtually every night, sometimes two or three times a night, with lines that are coming into my head. Today, I was thinking about the first person who was my age, who died, that I knew. One of my peers. It was a woman called Shirley Divers. Then a line came to me – which I know must come from somewhere else, I'll have to figure out where it comes from: "And now I shall never be young again, de dum de dum de dum de dum." It's almost iambic pentameter.'

One of his most popular poems, he said, is about two people. One has just died. The other 'is trying to call him back'.

Dennis said he was grateful for the second revelation – that creating art makes you happy. 'It has changed my life, discovering that I'm a poet,' he said. 'It makes me a little bit sad. Because perhaps I should have discovered that I was a poet in my twenties.'

Then he said: 'I am incredibly grateful to fortune, or to death, or life, or whatever it is, that I've been given yet another chance to live yet another life.'

And perhaps the fallout from the first revelation was the fuel for the second. Poets are very articulate about what they regret. And to write about regret, you have to find something you regret.

In his case, the money.

A woman appeared outside the Welshman's. 'How are you,' she asked.

'Very very well thank you I hope. At least I hope I am. I have been taught by the quacks to say, I am well, or at least I think I am.'

He wasn't. Shortly after I met him for the second time, he was walking through Dorsington, and he suddenly felt faint, and he had to lean against a tree. The cancer had spread to his lungs.

Soon afterwards, he died.

***

Josh Axelrad made hundreds of thousands of dollars by counting cards in casinos. But he couldn't deal with the lifestyle.

He wanted to have a less crazy life.

He decided to become a writer. Why not write a book about being a gambler? He sold a proposal for the book. His advance was $300,000. And then he hit a brick wall. He met with what Steven Pressfield would call resistance. Josh found himself with lots of time on his hands and no excitement.

He began to play online poker. Sometimes he played it in bed. Sometimes he won. But mostly, he lost. He was becoming pathological and self-destructive. It was simultaneously plunging him into despair and making him hugely excited.

He remembered a quote from David Foster Wallace. It was about how addiction presents itself as the solution to the problems it causes.

Josh lost more and more money. Tens of thousands of dollars. 'I was out of control, and I knew I was out of control, because I did not have the illusion that I was secretly good at this game. Intellectually, I knew I ought to be losing. So it was foolish to persist.'

But he persisted. 'And the more out of control I got, the more profound the feelings of exhilaration were.'

He said: 'Obviously it was disgusting. And just pathetic.'

This was not like losing money at the blackjack table. When that happened, 'I felt very sad. I wished I hadn't done it. But I didn't hate myself. I knew the decisions underlying that investment were rational.'

But losing at poker was different. 'I felt I could not, almost, look at myself in the mirror.'

Josh joined Gamblers Anonymous. He kept on playing online poker and losing money. Eventually he stopped. He'd lost $51,000. He wrote his book. It's called *Repeat Until Rich*.

***

Leon Max didn't marry Natasha. But Natasha introduced him to one of her friends, a Ukrainian model called Yana Boyko. Leon and Yana got married in 2014. At the reception, held at Easton Neston, Yana wore a grey dress from the Leon Max collection. The ninth Earl Spencer attended. Shortly afterwards, Yana gave birth to a boy. Leon Max says he's thinking about sending him to Stowe.

***

After writing *The Rational Optimist*, Matt Ridley wrote a book called *The Evolution of Everything*. It's a brilliant analysis of the way complex systems work, from the economy to life itself. 'If there is one dominant myth about the world, one huge mistake we all make,' wrote Ridley, 'it is that we all go around assuming the world is much more of a planned place than it is.'

***

Matt's Rock was eventually bought, debt and all, by the British government, for £1.4 billion. The bank was split into two parts – the 'good' half, which was an asset, and the 'bad' half, the half with the debt, which was obviously a liability.

Virgin Money bought the 'good' half of the bank for £747 million. A bargain. Even more of a bargain when you consider the fact that Virgin Money only actually paid £460 million. So where did the other £287 million come from? I went to see Jayne-Anne Gadhia, the CEO of Virgin Money, and she explained it to me. The £287 million came from Northern Rock's own capital. Virgin's £460 million enabled Northern Rock to release £287 million from a previously secure fund, because Virgin's £460 million changed Northern Rock's 'safety margin'. In other words, as soon as Virgin swapped one sort of money for another sort of money, the other sort of money became more valuable. Gadhia said: 'We've not taken money out of the bank at all that's come to our own coffers.'

So they bought a bank by using the bank's own money. They sort of helped a bank to buy itself, as long as it gave itself to them at the exact same time. A clever piece of financial engineering.

***

I met David Guetta in Bogota, Colombia, and we travelled to Peru in a private jet he'd hired for the day. He said he spent $20,000 every time he used a private jet, which was every two or three days. But the economics worked out pretty well. He was travelling around the world, performing in front of thousands, and sometimes tens of thousands, of people every few days. The cost of hiring the jet was incidental.

It felt like a dangerous contraption. Thin and elegant, it catapults you into the sky. We cruised at 40,000 feet. It felt a bit high for my liking. Guetta told me about co-writing, and co-producing, 'I've Gotta Feeling'. The song changed his life. It was a monster hit, of course. Afterwards, all sorts of pop stars wanted to work with him – Rihanna, Sia, Chris Brown, Snoop Dogg, Kelly Rowland, Nicky Minaj and Usher. Suddenly, he was in a different league. He could draw tens of thousands of people anywhere in the world.

He made millions. He made tens of millions. He bought homes in five places – England, France, California, Dubai and Ibiza. He would wake up somewhere in the world – it could be anywhere – and maybe he'd be in striking distance of one of his homes, and maybe not. He became disorientated. He started to have panic attacks. His marriage collapsed.

We flew over Siula Grande, the mountain Joe Simpson had climbed, before he fell into the crevasse.

At Lima, we got into another SUV. We talked about 'I've Gotta Feeling'.

Later, I would analyse it. I would listen to it over and over, read blogs, watch YouTube. The lyrics are cynical and brilliant. The song is about how partying can be addictive, and it also creates the *sensation* of what it feels like to be addicted to partying. It's a siren in both senses – a lure as well as a warning.

We got on a major highway. Our car was preceded by a police escort with its siren blaring. The police car was blasting through the traffic to create a lane for us. 'Do you feel like the president?' said Guetta.

He said: 'OK, so here's the thing. When you start, you look up. It's only positive energy. Your motivation is passion, love. But when you're at the top, what do you have?' Guetta paused. 'The only thing you have is the fear of going down.'

To our right were the barrios – the shanty towns that go on for miles. They were dotted with lights but soon, when we got to the poorer parts, they wouldn't be.

Ahead of us, the police siren blared.

***

Rick didn't make it. Soon after he lent me his copy of *Touching the Void*, he was walking along a busy road. Remember how I said that a busy road is just like a ledge? That's because the energy of a vehicle hurtling towards you can be as dangerous as the gravitational force that plummets you to the ground. So sometimes, when I think of Rick, I think of him stepping off a ledge. I try not to think of what happened next.

***

Remember that house? The house I've always coveted? The architectural gem, the mid-century porn mansion. Long and low, insolent and beautiful, the place the bad guy would live in a 1970s movie. Anyway, the house was put on the market. It was a million pounds more than I could afford. I posed as a buyer. Marched in. Talked in the way that rich people talk. Went for a viewing.

And . . . it was perfect. Walking around it, I felt lit up. It was my house! I wanted to fill it with my stuff! I went into one of the bedrooms. Saw the bedroom as it would be after I'd been living there for a while. The wet towels. The books, damaged with love like old teddy bears. The floor a rink of glossy magazines. The bed a trashed nest.

Which got me thinking.

***

My plane tilts downwards, towards Reykjavik, where I will stay, in other words where I will sleep. I will spend most of my time about fifty kilometres east of Reykjavik, across the tundra and into the mountains. My thoughts keep jumping forward to tomorrow morning. It will be dark. I will be driven across the tundra. The roads will be icy. There will be barriers and steep, icy drops. Eventually, we will arrive at our destination – the centre of discomfort. I can't remember the name of the place, but I imagine it as jagged, with big white slabs of ice. Wind scraping at my face and hands.

I'll be meeting a guy called Joe de Sena. I've been trying to imagine what it's like to *be* Joe de Sena. He's from what he describes as 'a Goodfellas neighbourhood in Queens'. He's Italian-American. He was the pool boy for an organised crime figure called Joe 'the Ear' Massino, so-called because, as a mob boss, he didn't want anybody to mention his name; you had to touch your ear instead.

The Ear gave Joe advice. When you do something, he said, you have to do it properly. No half-measures.

De Sena grew up and worked on Wall Street. He got rich. Then he had an idea that would make him even richer. He could see that everybody around him was getting addicted to comfort. He was getting addicted to comfort. It didn't make him feel good. 'We constantly try to make our lives easier, which only makes us weaker,' he says. And: 'We whine about even the most minor inconveniences.' This has 'turned us into plush-toy versions of ourselves – soft, overstuffed, and passive'.

De Sena's reasoning went something like this: if comfort makes us feel bad, what if the opposite is true? Does discomfort make us feel good? Turns out it does.

He had discovered a trick.

De Sena has said he agrees with Steven Pressfield. If you actively seek discomfort, if you learn to take hard choices, instead of easy ones, you will start to feel better.

You will be happier.

You will be more successful.

People want discomfort. They need it. You can sell it to them.

De Sena started a company and called it Spartan Race. He organises races, in which people experience extreme discomfort, all over the world.

He is Tom Sawyer. He is Felix Dennis. He is Howard Schultz. He is Jordan Belfort. Actually, he knows Jordan Belfort. 'I know Jordan,' he will tell me.

I look out of my window as the plane tilts downwards. Tundra with sharp white peaks. I run my tongue around my teeth, which I've had fixed.

I see my face reflected. For a moment I can visualise another version of myself. A person with grit. A person who does not want to be poor. A person who can get out of bed, who can walk to the desk, who can start to write.

It will come. One day, I will be inundated.

I look down. The tundra rises towards me.

Acknowledgements

I'd like to thank a few people who helped me along the way – my agent Antony Topping, my editor Michael Fishwick, and everybody at Bloomsbury, particularly Lauren Whybrow, Lilidh Kendrick and Jonny Coward. When I have an idea, I always run it past Antony to see if it's any good. He sees right into it straight away. He's great at making me laugh – particularly at myself. Michael was very patient. Lauren was brilliant and super-organised. She tried to stop me obsessing too much over the text. Lilidh was great at getting things done. Jonny was always ahead of the game. Thanks to Jo Forshaw for doing the audiobook.

There are lots of other people I'd like to thank. Jordan Belfort talked to me for hours and hours, and mesmerised and entertained me as well. Aaron Brown was great – he talked to me, he bought me dinner, he explained lots of things. There can't be many people in the world who understand money as well as he does. I would recommend his books *The Poker Face of Wall Street* and *Red-Blooded Risk*. This guy really understands the history of money.

Thanks, too, to George Cooper. His book *The Origin of Financial Crises* is superbly clear. He invited me into his office and talked to me for ages about it. Thanks to David Graeber for his book *Debt: the First 5,000 Years*, and, again, for talking to me. I'd like to thank David Wootton. His book *The Invention of Science* is the best thing I've read on the scientific revolution, and pretty much the best history book around – if I could only read one history book, it would be this one. Thanks to Matt Ridley for that great talk in Piccadilly. Thanks to David Gilmour of Fiji water, Howard

Schultz of Starbucks, Alan Sugar, Leon Max of Max Studio, Jayne-Anne Gahdia of Virgin Money, Joe Simpson, David de Rothschild, Joel Cohan, Nassim Nicholas Taleb, all of whom talked to me. Thanks to Rory Sutherland for inviting me to Nudgestock, and for introducing me to some brilliant people – like, for instance, Nobel laureate Richard Thaler. Not that Rory isn't a brilliant person himself. He is. Thanks to the late Felix Dennis for talking to me at his Warwickshire estate – and for trying to teach me to ride one of his Segway scooters. Thanks to Patrick Veitch for talking to me about horses and betting, and to Josh Axelrad for talking to me about card counting. Thanks to Jonathan Waters for his brilliant input about trading and more; thanks to Jonathan, and also Callum Murray, for being early readers. Thanks, too, to Robert Skidelsky for talking to me about Keynes, among other things. Thanks to Jonathan Waters for being my first reader. Finally: I didn't meet him, and I don't even know if this is his real name, but thanks to S.G. Belknap for his essay on pickup artists in *The Point magazine*.

A Note on the Author

William Leith has worked as a columnist and feature writer at the *Independent on Sunday*, the *Mail on Sunday* and the *Observer*. His writing spans a wide range of subjects, from food to celebrity, cosmetic surgery, fashion and film. He has written about kings in Africa, political tension in Palestine, nightlife in Bangkok, Hollywood film directors, diet gurus and the death of James Dean. He is the author of two previous books, *The Hungry Years* and *Bits of Me Are Falling Apart*.

A Note on the Type

The text of this book is set Adobe Garamond. It is one of several versions of Garamond based on the designs of Claude Garamond. It is thought that Garamond based his font on Bembo, cut in 1495 by Francesco Griffo in collaboration with the Italian printer Aldus Manutius. Garamond types were first used in books printed in Paris around 1532. Many of the present-day versions of this type are based on the *Typi Academiae* of Jean Jannon cut in Sedan in 1615.

Claude Garamond was born in Paris in 1480. He learned how to cut type from his father and by the age of fifteen he was able to fashion steel punches the size of a pica with great precision. At the age of sixty he was commissioned by King Francis I to design a Greek alphabet, and for this he was given the honourable title of royal type founder. He died in 1561.